"We have always tried to be guided by the basic idea that, in the discovery of knowledge, there is great entertainment."

—**Walt Disney,** on his belief that learning can be fun

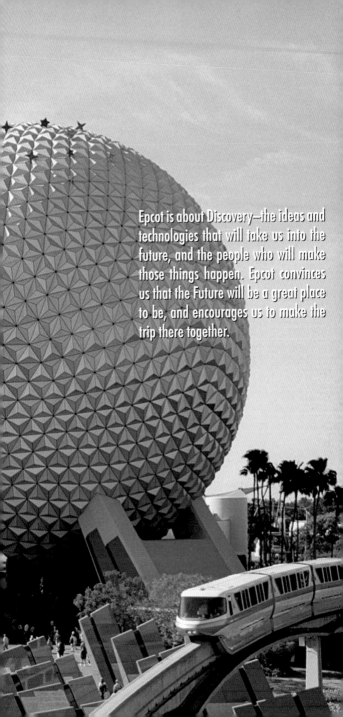

Epcot is about Discovery—the ideas and technologies that will take us into the future, and the people who will make those things happen. Epcot convinces us that the Future will be a great place to be, and encourages us to make the trip there together.

A New Variation on a Theme Park

The international spirit of the entrance to Epcot by Imagineer Herb Ryman

It's a Different Kind of Theme Park, Altogether

Epcot is the first park designed by the Disney Imagineers that is not based directly on the original Disney theme park—Disneyland in California. Our first Florida park, the Magic Kingdom—while maintaining its own identity and several differentiating factors—is clearly based on the model of Disneyland. For this reason, Epcot was a big risk for the company when it was undertaken as a full-fledged project in the mid-1970s. It was not known immediately how the public would react to a Disney park not based purely on fantastical stories and nostalgic visions. How would we address the inclusion of the Disney characters? Would the concept be as appealing without the fantasy of a Magic Kingdom park? Would a park modeled at least to some extent on the classic World's Fairs of the past maintain its appeal on a permanent basis?

These were all valid questions, and these and many others necessitated serious consideration. The team that was set after this task put forth a tremendous effort in the interest of broadening the definition of a Disney park. In the end, however, the concept thrived because it had originated from the creativity of one of the greatest visionaries and entertainers of the 20th century, and because of the organization he left behind.

Epcot is the embodiment of Walt Disney's last and possibly greatest dream. Opened in 1982, and originally named EPCOT Center, the Park embraces Walt's optimism that the greatest problems of our times could and would be solved through careful planning and thoughtful design. He had faith in the capabilities of people to generate new and better ideas and he felt that the public would respond once it understood the potential of those ideas.

A Positive Combination

Epcot puts forth the notion that the future is a positive place, where the wonders of science and technology will continue to improve the quality of life for people throughout the world. The two major sections of the Park, Future World and World Showcase, both work to establish this underlying theme. These two sections, however, actually began life as separate entities, being developed independently for potential applications as entertainment destinations at the Walt Disney World property.

The resulting park—its 260 acres coming in at more than twice the Magic Kingdom's approximately 120—combines these two ideas with aplomb, using a connecting thread coming from the basis of both stories. People are the core of the ideas—as the ones who will create the future and as the ones who will go there together. It makes for a park with a very grand vision, indeed. Once this connection was conceptualized, the two pieces were combined and became a much stronger idea than either one had been on its own.

The layout of the Park is a variation on the Magic Kingdom model as well. Rather than the hub-and-spoke park plan used since Disneyland, Imagineers had to come up with a new, but similarly effective, approach for Epcot. Since the two halves of the park still remained as distinct entities, they could not be merged into a single shape. For Future World, a modified hub-and-spoke remained, with all of the major elements falling around the perimeter outside the central plaza. World Showcase maintains a similarly clear layout, with all the nations arranged around a central lagoon perfect for transportation and show staging.

A model of an early version of the combined Park

Ep-what?

Walt Disney reveals his intentions for The Florida Project in a 1966 film.

The park was originally called EPCOT Center, its name an acronym for Experimental Prototype Community of Tomorrow. This was, of course, in recognition of its basis in Walt Disney's vision of the Florida property as a model for future community development, and of the Park as an expression of that vision. Even today, this name is very central to the identity of the Park.

The Park's name was changed in December 1993 in a nod to its evolving place in the public consciousness. While the name might have vexed those hearing it for the first time, once it had been around for a while, most visitors could tell you what the acronym stood for. By this time, EPCOT had become a recognizable tag, and the name had taken on a meaning that was identifiable to the average Guest. So, the name was simplified, but the core values underlying that name remain intact.

The original logo for the Park, dating back to when it was referred to as EPCOT Center. The Center designation referred to the fact that this Park was the focal point of the larger EPCOT—essentially the entire WDW property.

Concept art of Project X, as it was known then, by Herb Ryman

Words to Design By

Walt Disney once said in describing EPCOT, "I don't believe there's a challenge anywhere in the world that's more important to people everywhere than finding solutions to the problems of our cities." Walt shared this belief with his Imagineers and set them free to reimagine the city of the future. No facet was left untouched. No assumption went unchallenged. Walt knew that the best way to solve these problems was to start with a clean slate, "on virgin land," and build from the ground up. This was the original impetus for Walt Disney World in Florida.

Walt Disney didn't come to Florida just to build a theme park. He had done that before with Disneyland, and wasn't the type to just repeat his successes. He came to Florida to build a community—one that could serve as a model for other developments around the world.

Even though Walt never really built his city, per se, and Epcot as we know it is more a representation of that idea than a city unto itself, the entire WDW property does serve this function. The inventive transportation systems with monorails and PeopleMovers, the forward-thinking utility and land-use plans, the AVAC trash collection system at Magic Kingdom Park, and the water-control systems that allowed us to build in wetlands all carry on this dream.

Another view of Project X by Herb Ryman, this time focusing on the transportation systems

19

Walt Disney telling the world about his latest dream

Another Story to Tell

One of the favorite milestones in WDI lore is the famous (but, until recently, seldom seen) "EPCOT Film." Walt told the story of EPCOT to the cameras on a set at the studio lot dressed to look like the Florida Conference Room at WED Enterprises' Glendale headquarters, where the project was being planned. This amazing film—recorded in October 1966, just two months prior to Walt's death—succinctly captured a huge and grandiose vision in words and pictures. Walt's narration was written by Imagineering Show Writer Marty Sklar, who would one day head up the development of Epcot along with fellow Disney Legend John Hench as well as serving as WDI's Vice Chairman and Principal Creative Executive. This narration was combined with concept drawings and animations from his team of artists and designers to explain the idea of EPCOT to the public and, just as importantly, to the leaders of industry to whom Walt wanted to pitch this concept in order to gain their participation. This was a big part of how he saw the project functioning.

Walt was the consummate storyteller. It was the basis for everything he did in his long and illustrious career. In the early days he would talk his artists through the story of the films he wanted to make. He could always captivate an audience with a story, and put his skills to use to "sell" the concept of Epcot to the public.

A Work in Progress

An early vision of Epcot by Clem Hall

At the outset of the film, Walt acknowledges that the designs he was about to show were preliminary, and that anything and everything was subject to change before it was completed. The magic of Walt's design philosophy was that he was willing to let his cadré of designers explore multiple iterations of any idea, all in an effort to find the absolute *best* idea. This was to be the largest undertaking ever for the Disney company—and one of the biggest efforts ever by any corporate entity—so there was bound to be an extraordinary degree of diligence applied to the design process. That development work focused on several areas.

Perhaps foremost among these was the implementation of transportation networks that included new vehicles and systems. This subject had always been of interest to Walt, as evidenced by his fascination with trains that led in part to the construction of Disneyland and in his proposals of new systems such as the PeopleMover that made their first appearance there. In fact, many of the early concepts for Disneyland attractions focused on placing Guests into forms of transportation no longer in vogue or not yet invented. For EPCOT, the focus was on efficiency and safety, and relocation of elements to make for a more pleasing aesthetic to the cityscape.

Another area of interest was new thinking for commercial and residential spaces. He wanted to see a city center that was the hub for commerce as well as functioning as a vibrant meeting place. This city center was intended to be a showcase for the best that industry had to offer in new ideas, materials, and systems—and a test bed in which those developments could be introduced.

This city center was to be surrounded by a greenbelt that offered recreational opportunities and a planned break in the development to avoid the aesthetic blight of urban sprawl. The concept called for a different type of suburb, less detached from the city center because of the transportation system that linked the whole thing together. This was part of a larger picture of thoughtful environmental design to which Walt was entirely committed. These principles have been key to the development of WDW ever since its inception.

A Trial Run

As hard as it may be for us to imagine today, in the early days of Disneyland, there were significant doubts as to whether this concept would play on the East Coast. Even Walt wanted validation, so when the opportunity arose for him to design major attractions for the 1964-65 New York World's Fair, he was intrigued. Actually, he was more than intrigued—he jumped at the chance. He was able to create four of the largest

The iconic image of Spaceship Earth as rendered by Tom Gilleon captures the sense of classic World's Fairs.

and most technologically advanced attractions ever and try out his brand of entertainment on an entirely new audience—with funding from some of the largest corporations in the country. It was a perfect circumstance, and Walt didn't miss out on it. He even added to the obligation very late in the game, by adding the fourth attraction, "it's a small world," to the menu just nine months before the opening of the Fair.

The Disney attractions were a sensation at the Fair, attracting some of the longest lines, thereby convincing people both inside and outside the Disney organization that the concept was, indeed, viable. The advancements made at WED Enterprises during the development of these attractions changed the course of Disney parks from that point forward, and the effort added to the offerings at Disneyland almost immediately.

A Classic Combination . . . The roster of Disney attractions at the World's Fair

General Electric Progressland featuring Carousel of Progress

Walt Disney's Magic Skyway at the Ford Wonder Rotunda

Great Moments with Mr. Lincoln for the State of Illinois

"it's a small world" for UNICEF

Progressland at the 1964-65 New York World's Fair

The Payoff

The benefits of Disney's participation at the Fair are numerous. The knowledge gained from the implementation of new systems of crowd control, ride systems, and Audio-Animatronics influenced the art of Disney theme park design tremendously. The continual-motion audience movement systems from the cars of Magic Skyway to the Carousel of Progressland showed how effectively we could move large numbers of Guests through an attraction while maintaining control of their point of view and show timing. Great Moments with Mr. Lincoln brought Audio-Animatronics technology all the way from the charming, but comparatively simple, Enchanted Tiki Room—which had debuted just a year prior to the Fair—to the point where it was capable of fooling audiences into thinking there was an actor onstage portraying the 16th President. "it's a small world" introduced a high-capacity water ride and demonstrated an ability to capture a big idea in a charming show with a great song, and it has been a favorite at Disney Parks since making its way out West to Disneyland in 1966.

"it's a small world" at the 1964-65 World's Fair

The Only Constant Is Change

In the world of WDI design, that is. We feel that the only way to arrive at the best idea is by way of lots and lots of other ideas. We go through numerous design iterations before we decide that we've hit upon the right one. Epcot, in particular, went through a long and drawn-out process (pun intended) in order to achieve the difficult blending of its broad and varied themes. It is said that the Epcot concept went through 19 major design revisions on its way from inception to Opening Day. As with all of our work, Epcot continues to evolve today.

This last, most complete, and most definitive illustration of Epcot—a collaboration between Clem Hall and Bob Scifo—was painted based on a photo of the completed park model.

Early vision of Future World by Tom Gilleon

An early version of World Showcase, illustrated by Carlos Diniz

Yet another vastly different take on World Showcase, by John Hench

Multiple transportation systems overlap in this concept by Herb Ryman for Project X.

Moving Toward the Future

As with the earliest concepts for Disneyland, many of Walt's ideas for the city of the future that eventually became Epcot revolved around the subject of transportation. Whereas with Disneyland the intent was to bring back modes of transportation that were no longer available—and therefore carried value in a nostalgic setting—with EPCOT Walt truly wanted to apply creative thinking to generating new means of moving people in order to bring efficiency to the world's cities. It was a sincere study in industrial design applied to mass and individual people-moving systems, with the hope of benefiting real people in the real world.

Walt's city was envisioned as a place where the pedestrians never have to dodge delivery trucks because they've been routed underground before entering the city center. PeopleMovers would glide around on a second level in the city, connecting with monorails that shuttled commuters back out to the suburbs and to the theme park and resort hotels. The pedestrian spaces were separated and safe from moving vehicles. All the various groups would move around with relative ease because of this separation. This was the gist of the transportation design.

Many of these concepts had been explored in the development of the original Walt Disney World property. The monorail, in particular, fit into Walt's vision by separating groups of travelers with different departure and destination points in order to allow all of them to move with the least interference. The WEDWay PeopleMover put into Magic Kingdom Park's Tomorrowland soon after the Park opened was more of an attraction than a real transportation system, but it still demonstrated the concept. The back-of-house spaces keep support traffic diverted from the Guest traffic, provide service access for Cast Members, and maintain the quality of the show by minimizing visual intrusions. Even the Magic Kingdom's Utilidor system—employed here in a more limited capacity—serves to separate the support functions from the show. At Epcot, because of the increased size of the park and the ability to provide alternate transportation for Cast Members via perimeter roads, the tunnel system only runs under the central core, providing access to Spaceship Earth and the two Innoventions buildings.

A Monorail Runs Through It

It's no accident that the monorail passes right through the heart of this park. This connection not only transfers riders from the Transportation and Ticket Center, but gives them an overview of the Park on their way in. And it provides additional show value and kinetics for those already there.

The monorail has stood for years as a symbol of Disney futurism. Sleek, silent, efficient—monorails have been moving Guests to and fro since the Disneyland Tomorrowland renovation of 1959. Walt admired creative thinking in all aspects of planning, definitely including innovations in mass transit.

Monorail Yellow glides past Spaceship Earth.

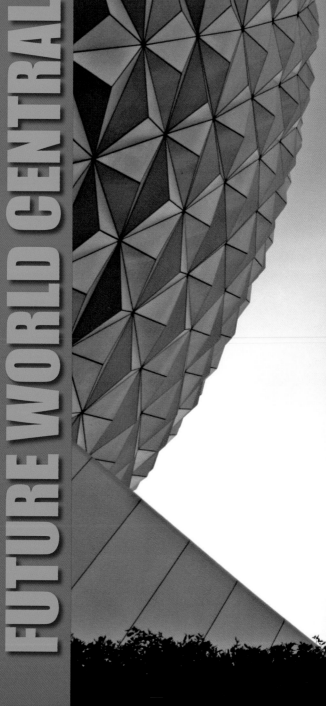

FUTURE WORLD CENTRAL

Future World offers a glimpse into a visionary future, led by innovations in the various fields of science and industry. The future is bright, learning is fun, and excitement is everywhere. The future is now!

Progress City

Another version of the park entrance by Herb Ryman

Future World is the part of the Park most closely derived from Walt's EPCOT concepts. This "permanent World's Fair," as it's been called, is intended to give Guests a look into what the future may hold in store for us—in our homes, at work, at play, and in the world around us. It's a showcase for the best future thinking in the realms of design, technology, communications, transportation, and more. It's an homage to the capabilities of people when they put their minds to tackling problems.

Future World, like the rest of Epcot, went through several major design changes on its way through the development process. It was once thought of as a stand-alone park, so merging it with World Showcase dictated some of those changes. The original conception relied heavily on the participation of corporate sponsors bringing their latest ideas to demonstrate them to the world. The current Park certainly makes use of this model to enrich our stories, but isn't as much of a real-world laboratory as was initially envisioned.

Early bird's-eye concept of an industrial park concept by George Rester

Conceptual bird's-eye view of Future World by Tim Delaney

The Big Picture

Future World, perhaps more than any other land in any Disney park, is founded on BIG ideas. It deals with real issues, bringing Disney storytelling to real-world subjects and themes. It takes its inspiration from Walt Disney's utopian visions, and turns them into a tangible representation of those fantastic dreams.

It can be seen as a further iteration of the Progress City concept originally introduced as an animated "model city" with the Carousel of Progress at Disneyland. This model—a portion of which can currently be seen from the Tomorrowland Transit Authority at Magic Kingdom Park—put forth a fully-dimensional rendering of Walt's grand scheme for a well-designed city, as it existed at that time. Of course, with Walt and his Imagineers continuing with their constant exploration of new ideas, the current state of the city of the future never stayed current for very long.

Future World also takes some of its physical design cues from the classic World's Fairs. The massive big-box pavilions, each housing a distinct sub-theme, as well as the park-like common spaces that thread them together, are certainly reminiscent of the landmark fairs of the 19th and 20th centuries. Even the inclusion of a large, unique, iconic structure such as Spaceship Earth owes much to the legacy of the icons of past Fairs such as the Perisphere and Trylon of the 1939-40 New York World's Fair, and the Unisphere at the 1964-65 New York World's Fair.

Another vision of Future World by Tim Delaney

Spaceship Earth

One of the first drawings of Spaceship Earth, by Herb Ryman

We're Having a Ball!

Spaceship Earth is Epcot's equivalent of Cinderella Castle at Magic Kingdom Park. It is a large, iconic structure that speaks volumes about the thematic intent of our Park. It is a "wienie" that draws us further into the Park to find out what else is there. At 180 feet tall, it's a recognizable landmark that can be seen from throughout the Park, and helps to maintain our sense of orientation as we make our way around.

Geodesic domes were the creation of Buckminster Fuller, the visionary architect and industrial designer responsible for many radical concepts. In his search for lightweight, stable, and mechanically efficient structures, he studied many different geometrical forms. He eventually settled on the tetrahedron-based spherical shapes because the tetrahedron resists external pressure more stongly than all other geometric forms, and the sphere is the strongest form in terms of resisting internal pressure—while enclosing the most space in relation to its surface area. He designed several geodesic domes, notably, the American pavilion at Expo '67 in Montreal, but was never able to achieve a completed sphere, as was done with Spaceship Earth.

32

The Spaceship Earth image was further developed in this concept by Herb Ryman.

UICK TAKES

• When engineers originally reported that a full geodesic sphere could not support itself structurally, Imagineering legend John Hench suggested an approach of treating the upper three-fourths and the lower fourth as separate pieces—one supported by a *table* at the top of the six legs and the other *hanging from the bottom* of that table.

• The hidden network of backstage corridors inside Spaceship Earth is understandably complicated, because of the shape of the building and the serpentine ride system. So much so that maintenance workers occasionally resort to drawing pencil lines on the walls (like bread crumbs) to find their way back to where they started!

• Spaceship Earth consists of two spheres. The inner sphere is the building membrane, sealed in a thick, black, rubber blanket for protection unlike any other building. The outer sphere is made up of 11,324 individual triangular panels made of an aluminum alloy—each one a custom fit.

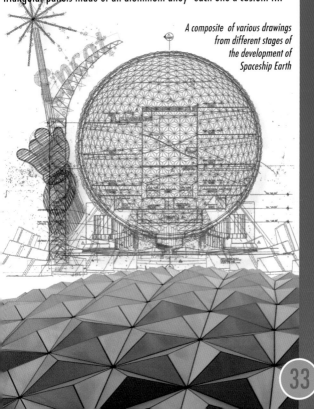

*A composite of various drawings
from different stages of
the development of
Spaceship Earth*

Spaceship Earth

All Aboard

Spaceship Earth inspirational concept by Tom Gilleon

Besides having developed the architectural form of the geodesic sphere, Buckminster Fuller also coined the term, "Spaceship Earth," making the merging of these two concepts in Epcot's signature attraction an apt fit. He first used the term in his seminal 1969 work, "Operating Manual for Spaceship Earth," in which he put forth a vision of the people of this planet as crew members on a cosmic voyage—bound by our shared destiny, moving toward our common future. He generated some of the earliest concepts of sustainable living, of responsible use of resources, and design with an eye toward its long-term implications.

These concepts are clearly central to the core philosophies of Epcot, and they stuck with Imagineer John Hench after a conversation he had with Fuller in the 1970s. They form the basis for much of Future World, with Spaceship Earth as the headliner. Our attraction takes as its theme the history of human communications. It makes sense as an iconic attraction here, because communications are the basis for everything else that comes after—it's how we retain and pass along knowledge, it's how we work together to further that knowledge, and it's how we share the benefits of this knowledge going forward.

Concept for Spaceship Earth with ride system by Jim Dow

Fast Backward

Spaceship Earth handles its educational duties in a way that should be familiar to those who've followed Disney for years. This is the concept of inspiring people about the future by drawing a connection to the past. In shorts such as *Toot, Whistle, Plunk and Boom* and the entire *Man in Space* series, Walt begins his stories by going way back in time—to caveman days, actually—to demonstrate the origins of the subject at hand. In this

Conceptual image by Tom Gilleon

way, we as the viewer can draw a conclusion as to where the topic is going by projecting forward along the path that has been laid out before us. It's a marvelous storytelling technique that helps to take a topic that might have the potential to be rather abstract and make it familiar, instead.

We have scenes involving cavemen painting on the walls of their caves, Michelangelo painting the ceiling of the Sistine Chapel, the development of Gutenberg's first printing press, and the 20th-century paperboy hawking the day's news from the sidewalk. All of these things pave the way for the scenes that follow, in which Imagineers extrapolate the technologies to a logical or at least fanciful conclusion.

These grand visions of a worldwide communications infrastructure are intended to imagine for us the ways in which these emerging technologies will continue to bring us together in the future.

Spaceship Earth has quite possibly the most distinctive shell of any Disney attraction anywhere in the world.

Worldly Waters

At the center of Millennium Plaza lies a fountain that expresses much of what Epcot is all about—the World Fellowship Fountain. While it adds to the kinetics of the plaza all through the day and looks wonderful going through its periodic shows and lit for nighttime visibility, it really carries more meaning than that. This fountain was dedicated during a ceremony at the opening of the Park presided over by Lillian Disney, Walt's widow. At this ceremony, representatives from 23 countries brought water from 23 rivers and lakes from around the world to feed the fountain and build its foundation as a gathering point for the world community. This message, tying together the people of the world with a view toward commonalities and shared aspirations, serves as the perfect bridge between the concepts of Future World and World Showcase.

Surprise by Design

Sometimes we put into the parks little hidden gems that don't get a lot of attention or capture a large audience for a great deal of time, but that catch people off guard and add a little element of surprise to their day. An example of this is the talking drinking fountain in Millennium Plaza. This element, added during the 1994 renovation of the area, is a simple little gag that really does come at you when you least expect it.

Fiber Optical Effects

One of the features added to the plaza during the 1994 redevelopment was the fiber-optic patterns worked into the paving near the entrance to the Innoventions buildings. This technique, which is a labor-intensive process owing to the sheer number of fiber-optic points and the necessity of embedding them cleanly in the base material, was later used as the basis for the swirling optical effect on the main marquee for The Twilight Zone™ Tower of Terror at the Disney Studios.

No Raining, No Pouring

To avoid soaking Guests during a shower, Spaceship Earth is fitted with a gutter system at the belt line of the sphere that gathers the water and funnels it to World Showcase Lagoon.

A Moving Image

One of our core principles of design for our exterior spaces is to bring the spaces to life through the inclusion of kinetic elements that add motion and action within the field of view. For each area, we try to find the appropriate pieces with which to accomplish this. For Future World, in addition to the fountain, we chose to include motorized whirligigs and playful, sculptural spinners rendered in glossy materials and paint finishes.

37

Concept for Innoventions Plaza by James Wong

Innovation + Invention = Innoventions

Innoventions is the part of the park in which we bring the future closer to the Guest. While it is thrilling and exciting to see visions of a future that might be decades or more away, the overall experience of a day in Future World would be a bit hollow if all it entailed were these far-off possibilities. Innoventions makes the future tangible, tactile, and fun. It's an opportunity to see how new advances in the technologies of various industries are going to affect the way we live our lives, do our jobs, and spend our playtime—in the near term.

It is inspired by the energy of a modern consumer-electronics expo, where we find something new and fresh around every corner. Exhibits are presented by some of the leading companies and trade organizations in all of modern industry. Our exhibits are designed to be active, enjoyable, informative, and clearly associated with our everyday lives. In this way, Innoventions takes on an overall story that is connected to—but also distinct from—the discreet story lines necessary to sustain each exhibit.

Quick sketches by D. Purcell explore composition options for Innoventions

New Stuff Is an Old Idea

Innoventions directly fulfills one of Walt Disney's original goals for EPCOT. He always saw his city of the future as a place where the leaders of world industry could showcase their newest and most cutting-edge technologies so that visitors could get a glimpse into the ways in which industrial progress would shape their lives. Early Disneyland was filled with similar exhibits—designed by Disney, funded by corporate sponsors—extolling the virtues of aluminum and chemistry and bathrooms of the future. He always felt that the inventiveness of modern industry would solve many of the world's problems through new ideas and innovative design. He was fascinated with the ongoing development of these ideas and wanted to share his enthusiasm with his Guests.

A Familiar Face (or Name, Anyway)

The host of Innoventions, Tom Morrow 2.0, is named in an inside joke referring back to the Audio-Animatronics host of the long-gone Mission to Mars attraction at Magic Kingdom Park.

Concept by Tim Delaney for the original Communicore

The Next Generation

Innoventions is an evolution of the attraction that first occupied this space when the Park opened in 1982, known as Communicore. Communicore followed a similar model of individual pods telling stories of technologies rapidly advancing in the world around us. Where it differed was in the nature of the technology under review. It was less specific in terms of a real-world application, less tied to a specific corporate sponsor, and less imminent insofar as when we might actually see these technologies come to fruition. In the course of our constant efforts to review the parks and look for opportunities to improve (or *plus*) the show, we saw the need to bring something closer to the Guest's world, and saw this facility as the prime place to do it. The scale of the spaces makes it possible to regularly update them in the interest of timeliness. Shows at Innoventions feature technologies and ideas that are often "leading edge."

39

FUTURE WORLD EAST

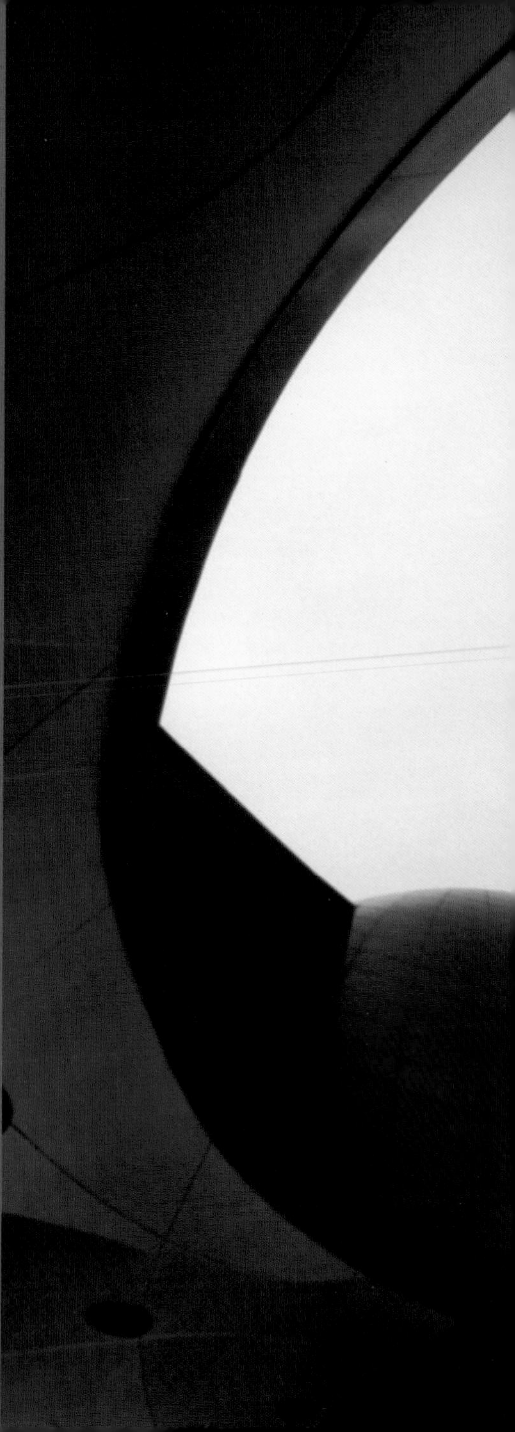

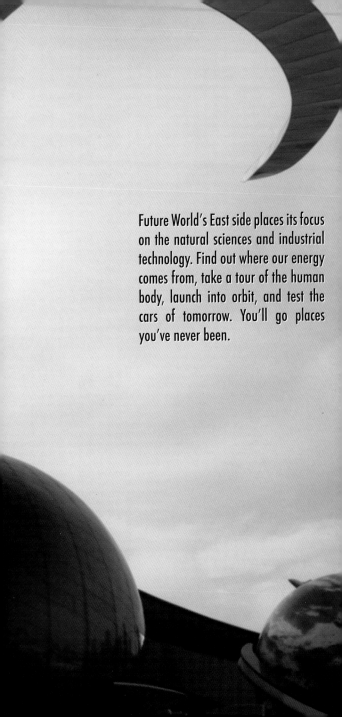

Future World's East side places its focus on the natural sciences and industrial technology. Find out where our energy comes from, take a tour of the human body, launch into orbit, and test the cars of tomorrow. You'll go places you've never been.

Exterior rendering by Bill Sully

High-Energy Design

The Universe of Energy, with the attraction Ellen's Energy Adventure, is a pavilion that really "puts its money where its mouth is" by generating a portion of its energy requirements from the large array of solar cells that cover its roof. It's one of the first things a Guest takes note of when viewing the structure, which is clearly the intent.

Once inside we are taken on a journey through the history of fossil fuels and alternative sources of energy by a roster of favorite television and movie personalities. We see how the development of these tremendous sources of energy has shaped our past, and how they will continue to shape our future. The show carries an ambitious goal—that of helping Guests take a serious look at the many faces of energy, stressing the realities and responsibilities we all must face concerning our vital resources, and optimistically presenting energy options for the future.

The show tackles this subject—which runs the risk of being somewhat dry and heavy—with humor and an attitude that knowing your stuff can be fun. By placing the title character, Ellen, into a recognizable game show setting, and playing off her insecurities regarding her friends, we give the effort a goal and make the task into a game. A spoonful of sugar, one might say. All the information is still given out during the course of the show, but you didn't even know it was good for you, did you?

In this case, the use of well-known actors allows us to make use of their established personality types and get right into our story with the least amount of explication. The audience already knows what each of these performers typically brings to their roles, so they can make the connection quickly to their part in this show.

QUICK TAKES

• The roof of the attraction is covered with two acres of photovoltaic cells, providing 15% of the power needed to run the attraction inside. There are 80,000 cells, producing a peak output of about 70,000 watts of direct current, which is then converted into alternating current for use inside.

• The building is placed within the park so that the solar cells get optimal exposure to the Sun, which also leads to the wedge-shaped profile of the roof—so that the collectors are angled even more directly toward it.

• Theater 1 contains three 70mm projection screens, each measuring 157 feet wide by 32 feet high. The theater seating then separates into six 97-passenger vehicles that travel through the rest of the pavilion to deliver the Guests to the show.

• Disney artists have provided their audiences with some of the most striking (for their time) visualizations of dinosaurs—dating back to the "Rite of Spring" segment in *Fantasia* in 1940, through the Universe of Energy Audio-Animatronics dinosaurs of 1982, and on to the amazing computer-generated stars of *Dinosaur* in 2000.

Background illustration by Bill Anderson and dinosaur maquettes by George Snowdon and Blaine Gibson

This early concept by Herb Ryman is far-removed from the golden dome that was built.

A Healthy Idea

There was practically from the beginning a placeholder on the various Epcot park plan for a "Life and Health" pavilion. While it was clear that this concept needed to be a part of Future World, this is one over which Imagineers really struggled to find a suitable storytelling technique or technology to apply. We only want to use the best possible means to tell our stories, so this project sat on the back burner for many years—so many years that even now more than two decades after it opened many Imagineers who were around at that time still refer to it reflexively as "Life & Health."

When the right technology did present itself—namely in the form of the simulator system for the signature attraction Body Wars—the Imagineers were ready, and had plenty of other ideas with which to surround that E-Ticket attraction. The accompanying Cranium Command theater show, *The Making of Me* film, and the stage for the Anacomical Players completed the menu. They took these ideas and placed them into a 100,000-square-foot dome, with a framework reminiscent of the natural structures of crystals and plant cells. The dome is 250 feet in diameter and 65 feet high.

The motif of the central area of the pavilion is that of a stylized county fair, appropriate given the active and healthful subject matter. It's bright, fresh, friendly, and intentionally not as techno-heavy as the rest of Future World. For this story, we want the Guest to feel entirely comfortable in a human-oriented space. There's plenty of time for the technological side when we get over to Body Wars!

This show concept illustration by Frank Armitage clearly foretells…

44

… the finished look seen inside the body probe.

Section view through pavilion by Greg Wilzbach

A New Adventure Thru Inner Space

We Imagineers love to refer back to the classics when we develop new attractions. More than that, we never let a good idea go away entirely—and often look for ways to apply new technology to a given story to make it even better. Adventure Thru Inner Space was a well-liked attraction during its stay at Disneyland from 1967 to 1986. This clever OmniMover attraction purported to shrink the passengers down to microscopic size to show them a fantastic view of the inner workings of an atom. Certainly the idea of using microscopic scale to make complex subjects clearly visible would be a great fit at a pavilion devoted to life and health. And a newly available simulator technology offered the ability to make the show even more immersive.

Comic Relief

Humor is certainly the order of the day at Wonders of Life's other key attraction, Cranium Command. This clever little show puts the Guest into another part of the human body—this time the brain itself. The film was directed by Kirk Wise and Gary Trousdale, who would go on to direct *Beauty and the Beast*, *The Hunchback of Notre Dame*, and *Atlantis: The Lost Empire* for Feature Animation. Kirk Wise also voices the Hypothalamus, and Gary Trousdale's name makes a cameo as the moniker of an enthusiastic recruit. General Knowledge is voiced by Corey Burton, the current voice of Captain Hook, among other characters.

These early concept sketches of Buzzy by X. Atencio bring to mind several points. First, they show the distance our concepts can travel from first sketch to finished piece. Second, they demonstrate the value of having animators such as X. on the team at Imagineering, as so many of the shows we design require characters to be designed to carry them. And lastly, it shows how broadly talented he was. X.—who began his Disney career as a story artist with Walt at the animation studio—went on to work as a Show Writer at WDI and actually wrote "Yo Ho (A Pirate's Life for Me)" and "Grim Grinning Ghosts," two of our most beloved songs.

45

The hulking form of Universe of Energy is softened by the rainbow color palette.

A Bright Future

During the 1996 rehab that brought Ellen's Energy Adventure to Future World, the Imagineers rethought the exterior color treatment. Our resident color expert, John Hench, selected the warm, prismatic colors to evoke the image of a rainbow and bring to the pavilion the sense of optimism that permeates our vision of tomorrow. The rainbow is particularly apropos in *light* of the solar panels gathering sunshine on top of the building.

Color Is Key

Even an individual attraction facade can have a "wienie." In the case of Mission: SPACE, it's the large, reddish orb that draws us in to the entry point of the queue. This element also serves as an accent piece to the wash of gleaming steel, aluminum, and plaster that forms the bulk of the attraction facade. Its finish is very critical to the materials palette visible at the front of this wonderful architectural statement. This sphere is representative of our destination of Mars—hence the bright, red color—but needs to maintain a distinctive and otherworldly look. So, a very special color-shifting paint was applied, at a cost of over $800 a gallon!

Future World solar bench in design-development drawing by Jim Heffron and as a finished piece built by Doug Esselstrom.

A Strong Bench

This clever little piece placed into Future World in 1995 is just the sort of detail WDI loves to add to the parks. Here's a bench designed to be a self-contained solar-powered comfort station for a weary Guest. It plays beautifully into the technological bent of this side of Future World. The solar panels on top gather energy to power the cooling fans and the nighttime lighting. The design was done to a reasonable level of detail, with dimensions and material call-outs to lead the fabrication effort, and the entire thing was built single-handedly in the model shop by Imagineer Doug Esselstrom. This demonstrates the capabilities of our Production Design and Fabrication disciplines.

Splashdown

In the heat of Florida, an opportunity to cool down in a cool spray of water is always welcome. WDI works with park operators to determine the locations for places to put water elements like these where they are most needed. We look for locations with high-traffic patterns, available space, and special circumstances such as kids waiting for other family members on a given attraction. This fountain takes its design direction from the overall geometry of Future World East.

47

Walt on the set of one of the introductory segments from Man in Space

A Man in Space

Walt was fascinated by the exploration of space. He was a champion of the space race of the 1950s and 1960s, always working to portray space travel in his parks, and even on television. In 1955 he presented the first of a series of episodes of the Disneyland TV show designed to help the American public *gravitate* toward a positive view of the great effort that would take mankind to its final frontiers. These programs, *Man in Space*, *Man and the Moon*, and *Mars and Beyond*, were directed by animator Ward Kimball, one of Walt's fabled Nine Old Men. Ward was a railroad enthusiast like Walt, but knew nothing, really, about the science of space exploration. Walt reasoned that this would make him the perfect foil to lead viewers through the complex concepts as he would be learning right along with them!

5, 4, 3, 2 . . . Hold Countdown!

Space is a natural extension of the themes of Future World. However, the concept proved to be one of the most elusive of all for the Imagineers. Over the years, several attraction ideas have been conceived and developed, only to eventually fall short in terms of storytelling or the technology available at the time. These included various forms of blastoffs, space walks, and interplanetary encounters. A good story never goes away entirely, however, and the lure of space travel proved too great to ignore. When the possibility arose to use NASA-grade centrifuge technology to replicate the physical sensations of space travel, and imaging technology came along to allow for a realistic view in such cramped quarters, the Mission: SPACE project was launched. Imagineers worked with NASA scientists and astronauts to envision realistic space travel as it might exist 20–30 years in the future.

This concept by Greg Pro captures the excitement of the meteor-shower scene.

A New Spin

At Imagineering, our approach never revolves around technology for the sake of technology—but rather technology applied in the service of great storytelling. While the new implementation of the centrifuge certainly provided all of the thrills we needed to replicate the sensations of space travel here on Earth, there still needs to be a backstory that gives you a reason for going. And so, the International Space Training Center (ISTC) was born. This concept for the training site of a fictional near-future space agency serves as the launching point for that story.

In the lobby of the ISTC we learn about the milestones that have occurred in space travel through the course of real history as well as during the intervening years. We prepare for our future flight by participating in a training mission. Our vehicle, the Space Shuttle X1, is an extrapolation of existing technology developed by Imagineers in consultation with NASA designers. This measure of authenticity pursued by the Imagineers permeates the attraction and ensures that the audience is never taken out of the fantasy by a conflict of story or design.

Space Shuttle X1 concepts
by Luc Mayrand

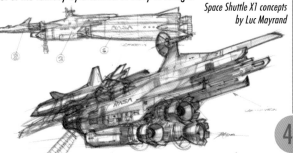

49

Cramped Quarters

The design of the passenger cabins for Mission: SPACE was a critical part of the project effort. The spatial and other constraints were very difficult to reconcile with the show requirements.

The limits on size and weight were laid out for the designers by the engineering team. Considering that the capsules had to provide audio, video, control systems, force feedback in the joysticks, transducers for the bass rumble under the seats, lighting, ventilation, safety restraints, and show graphics, this was quite a problem to solve.

We Spaced Out in Class

It is very important that all of our attractions at Epcot feature both entertainment and learning opportunities. This is borne out in the forecourt, where a planetary sculpture garden displays information about all of man's efforts at lunar exploration as well as quotations of those who've led the race.

FRONT ELEVATION

Lunar sculpture elevation by Victor Post

The Show Must Go On, and On, and On...

Mission: SPACE offers a great illustration of a post-show. Post-show spaces extend the themes of a show beyond the attraction itself, allowing the experience to continue for those who've ridden the attraction, or begin for those who have bypassed the ride. Post-shows can take on many formats. This one is focused on interactive experiences and group games that build on the stories of space exploration and teamwork that are the centerpiece of the ride-adventure.

Post-show concept by Chris Turner

Riding High

The complicated ride vehicle of Test Track speeds into view.

Disney parks have always featured rides, even before the parks existed! Even the never-built precursor to Disneyland—the idea for the Riverside Drive park across from the Studio lot—was concepted around a series of rides that Walt wanted to offer to his Guests. There were to be trains, riverboats, and old-fashioned horse-drawn trollies—all of which eventually made their way into Disneyland. That legacy has been built upon ever since, and continues to this day.

Since then, however, ride development and engineering has become a far more sophisticated process. WDI's Show/Ride Engineering department features multiple engineering disciplines—mechanical, electrical, hydraulic, and others—combined with software developers, computer modellers, and any other type of designer needed to produce a given ride system.

Ride systems are like any other technology we employ. They are of no use to us if they do not further our stories. They can be part of the placemaking, they can offer excitement and the thrills of speed or altitude, and they assist us with maintaining our show timing and the direction of the audience's focus. We work very hard to match our ride systems properly with each story concept.

Mission: SPACE's simulators, the wonderful flight system of Soarin', and the high-speed and highly complicated test vehicles of Test Track are a few prime examples of their work here at Epcot. At other parks, we find OmniMovers such as at The Haunted Mansion, rugged safari vehicles at Disney's Animal Kingdom, Enhanced Motion Vehicles such as those at the Indiana Jones™ Adventure at Disneyland and Dinosaur at Disney's Animal Kingdom, and the free-ranging honey pots of Pooh's Hunny Hunt at Tokyo Disneyland.

51

Exterior concept for Journey Into Imagination with Figment by Dan Goozee

You *Can* Judge a Building by Its Cover

Future World in Epcot, unlike most of our other park settings, isn't a theatrically-based recreation of a particular time and place, however fanciful. Rather, Future World is a collection of elements that represent, in abstract terms, the ideas and concepts upon which Epcot was founded. The materials palette, the massive forms of the buildings themselves, and the specific choices of what elements of the show might make their way outside all work to define the architectural statements.

So, here we see the flowing waveforms of roofline of The Living Seas as well as the waves crashing on the rocks in front, the soaring orbital shapes of Mission: SPACE, and the functional and symbolic solar cells on the roof of Universe of Energy. We have the prism-like glass pyramids of Journey Into Imagination with Figment that capture the full spectrum of the rainbow. The cars screaming around the front of the Test Track building and the greenhouse roof peeking over the top of The Land demonstrate the purpose of each of those structures. The Wonders of Life pavilion is fronted by the 76-foot-high Tower of Life based on the helical structure of DNA. Surely the most striking example of this design approach is Spaceship Earth itself, poetically capturing a vision of our planet in its shimmering metallic form.

THE LIVING SEAS

Careful Planning

Test Track exterior elevation by James Wong

While some of these details are quite obvious, others are fairly subtle, and difficult to make out from the typical Guest's point of view. The plan view of Test Track—the footprint of the building that one would see from the air—is circular. This simple shape is intended to be vaguely reminiscent of a wheel, which ties well both to Test Track, the current experience, and to World of Motion, the original attraction in the space. From the air, the curvilinear facades of The Living Seas create an overall form that is similar to a tide pool with swirling eddies. The Universe of Energy is sited on the park plan so that it maintains a strong southern exposure to maximize the effectiveness of its solar cells.

Mission: SPACE wears its subject matter on its face as in this concept by Eric Heschong.

On the Fast Track

Concept illustration of high-speed loop by Albert Yu

The development of Test Track shows us the extreme lengths (and speeds) to which Imagineers will go to research their work. The team of Imagineers assigned to produce this 1998 replacement for the original World of Motion spent significant time at an actual automotive proving ground. In partnership with General Motors, the presenting sponsor for this high-speed ride through the rigorous circuit, Imagineers studied extensively what it takes to make vehicles roadworthy, in order to impart that experience to our Guests. The team was particularly inspired by the "HYGE" Sled (Hydraulically-Controlled Gas-Energized) that is used in place of actual cars for the purposes of high-speed crash testing.

That's Some Ride

The technology employed in Test Track rivals that of any theme park attraction ever produced. Each car carries onboard more than enough processing power to run the Space Shuttle. It's a very complex effort to manage each car through its paces, at vastly varying speeds (including a complete stop), all the while maintaining the proper intervals between vehicles. Each vehicle is equipped with onboard audio-visual systems. This vehicle, combined with the many complicated special effects and show elements made Test Track one of WDI's most challenging achievements.

Interior ramp concept by Albert Yu

(VERY) QUICK TAKES

• The chassis of each vehicle is made entirely of composite materials, meaning there is no steel between the front and rear wheels.

• Each vehicle carries three onboard computers that combine to exceed the processing power onboard the Space Shuttle.

• Each vehicle generates 250 horsepower, more than most passenger cars on the road today.

• Test Track is the fastest Disney attraction anywhere in the world, attaining a top speed of 65 miles per hour.

Vehicle concept designs by Albert Yu

An Epcot Kind of Thrill

Epcot has a very different character from that of our other parks. While it's certainly possible to craft a compelling thrill attraction for Epcot, you have to go about it in a different way, for all of our attractions at Epcot need to have a story connection to the thrills. There will always be an informative aspect underlying all the shows that we do here. In the case of Test Track, the story gave us *license* to go with a more thrilling treatment while still remaining true to our subject matter. The approach in Test Track was instrumental in the development of Mission: SPACE and Soarin'.

Concept by Albert Yu for a thrilling Test Track scene

55

Kidcot

This Kidcot logo, developed by WDI Graphic Designer Jason Grandt, embodies the exuberance of youth and the wonderful optimism a child brings to a view of the future. It's very important that we have elements in the Park that reach children directly. By enabling them to play as they learn, we capture one of Walt's core beliefs—that learning can and should be fun.

Child's Play

One of the central themes of Walt Disney's body of work is the notion that learning can be fun and entertaining. We see this demonstrated in projects ranging from the classic *Toot, Whistle, Plunk and Boom* animated short to the *Man in Space* series from the 1950s to the hilarious Goofy shorts intended to teach children concepts such as safe driving and good sportsmanship. The True-Life Adventure films are another example of this concept applied to educational subjects. Walt was a naturally curious person who enjoyed learning, so he wanted to impart this enjoyment to others. Clearly, Epcot wouldn't exist in its current state if this idea were not a closely held truism for the entire Disney company.

At Epcot, more than any other Disney park, our stories rely on a foundation of information. The pavilions of Future World are all intended to convey information about a field of study deemed important to us as people on this planet. Of course Disney is, at heart, an entertainment company, so we develop stories for these pavilions that entertain while they inform.

Kids who make the rounds of all of the Kidcots in Future World can add elements to this card to mark their achievement.

Goofy teaches us about automotive physics at Test Track in this graphic by Jason Grandt.

Designing with Character

In Future World, Kidcots employ well-known characters to instruct children in the basics of the technologies and sciences on display. This does several things for us. It creates an image that is immediately familiar and inviting to the children who are its intended audience. It gives us a voice to use in developing the content—providing a point of view that these well-known personalities might bring to a particular topic. It also allows us the opportunity to impart humor and make the subject fun for those young Guests.

As WDI designers, we rely on these story cues to give us our direction and help us to make choices as we develop our designs. For example, a character might suggest a specific visual style and/or color palette, derived from his or her environment or individual design characteristics. It might dictate a distinct choice of words in any accompanying text, as each character brings with it its own vocabulary and manner of speech. It can also give us a framework by which to integrate the exhibit into its park surroundings.

So, the choice of character is very helpful to us as we go further into the design process with that character as the center of the story, but it also means that we have to be very careful in making the choice of which character(s) to use in the first place. The characters from *Finding Nemo* are an obvious selection for The Living Seas, but using Goofy for Test Track might not be so obvious. It requires a real exploration of the background of each character and the ways in which its personality has been established in the past.

Kidcot graphic by Jason Grandt

Timon and his buddy, Pumbaa, make great spokes-animals for Kidcot at The Land, where the story is all about bugs—one of Pumbaa's favorite topics!

BUGS ARE GREAT

AND **TASTY** TOO!

Insects play an important part in keeping plants healthy and happy. Using good bugs to control pests helps us cut back on pesticides, and that's good for all of us.

57

FUTURE WORLD WEST

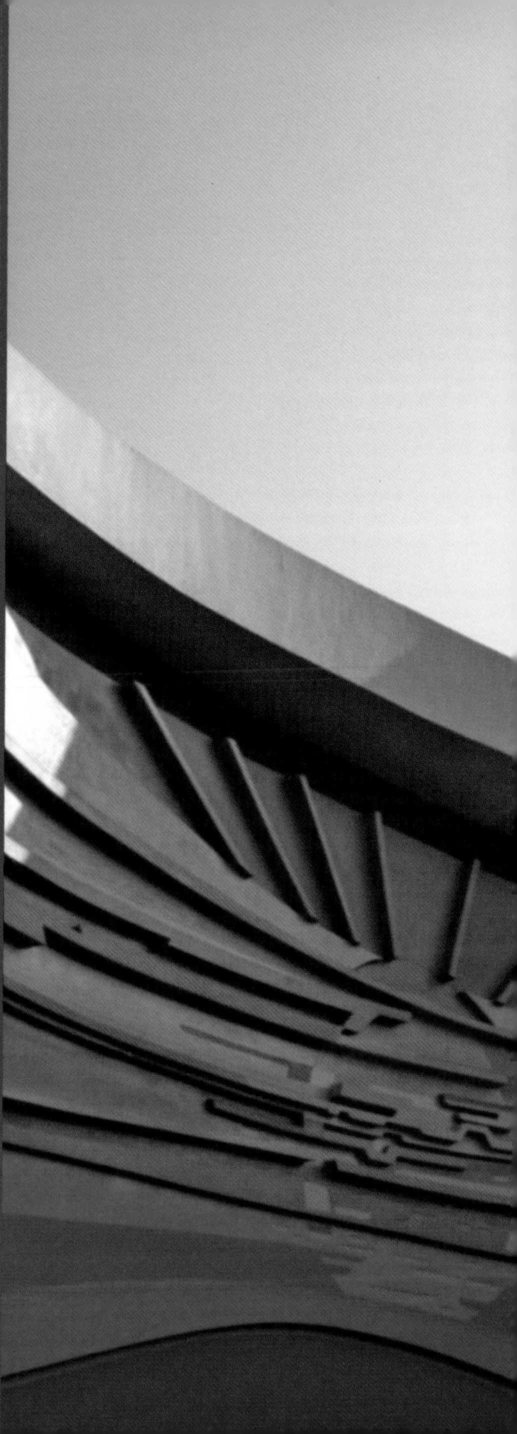

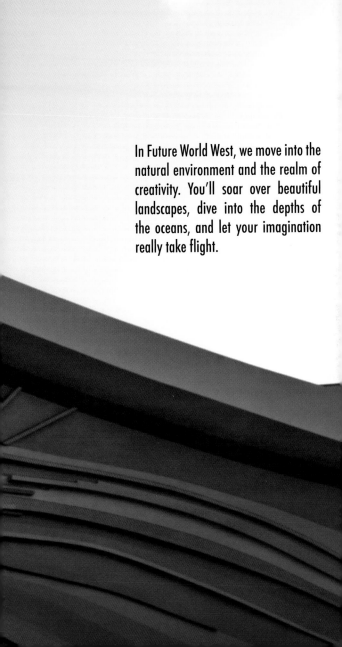

In Future World West, we move into the natural environment and the realm of creativity. You'll soar over beautiful landscapes, dive into the depths of the oceans, and let your imagination really take flight.

The Living Seas

Top Tank

Concept by Tim Delaney for the exterior of The Living Seas

The Living Seas has been a favorite attraction since its debut in 1986. The adventurous place making of the pavilion and the wonder of live aquatic animals have given this place a special allure. Because of the way we see the world, Imagineers believe that the best way to learn something is through experience. With that in mind, we believe that the best way to teach someone about a given place is by taking them there and showing it to them rather than just telling them about it. So, in order to learn about the oceans and aquatic life, we make the trip deep below the surface to the oceanic research center SeaBase Alpha.

When introduced to the incredible characters from the Walt Disney Pictures presentation of a Pixar animated film, *Finding Nemo*, the Imagineers saw an opportunity to tap into a brand-new group of storytellers who could take our Guests to school on the amazing oceanic world that is their home. We looked for ways to integrate these characters into the show in a way that would enhance the important environmental message of the pavilion. Now, they welcome us to SeaBase Alpha and serve as our guides. Mr. Ray returns to his familiar position as teacher; Bruce, Chum, and Anchor tell us about sharks and turtles; and Dory passes along whatever bits of information she can remember.

LIFE SUPPORT SYSTEMS LS86

This phrase, found on the walls of SeaBase Alpha, refers to the 1986 opening of the attraction.

Characters like Bloat are the perfect spokesfish for our discovery of the depths of the sea.

Talking Turtle

One of the most intriguing additions to The Living Seas is Turtle Talk with Crush, your opportunity to meet and interact with the scene-stealing surfer-dude star of *Finding Nemo*. This experience is intriguing as much for what it portends for the future as for what it represents on its own merits. Turtle Talk is a component of WDI's Living Characters program. This is a concerted effort to bring to life the beloved characters our Guests know and love from the vast and constantly growing Disney film library and place them into our parks in new and different ways.

The first fruits of this effort were realized with a very popular Stitch phone installed as a test in Disneyland's Tomorrowland in 2002. The program also produced Lucky the Dinosaur, a walk-around performer able to roam the parks and respond to Guests and the commands of his handler. Lucky has appeared at Disney's California Adventure and Disney's Animal Kingdom and was an "Opening Day" attraction at Hong Kong Disneyland in September 2005.

Living Characters can take numerous forms and can communicate with Guests in countless ways. The point of this program is to explore all of those options. Even we don't know what form the next Living Character might take.

Little dudes have the opportunity to talk to one of their favorites.

QUICK TAKES

• At its debut in 1986, The Living Seas boasted the world's largest aquarium, at over 5.7 million gallons. Its diameter—200 feet—is greater than that of Spaceship Earth.

• The tank is home to over 3,000 sea creatures representing 200 different species of aquatic life, including sharks, rays, dolphins, sea turtles, parrotfish, angelfish, snappers, and more.

East vs. West

Future World East presents chiseled edges and angular forms.

There are subtle but important differences in the area development of the two halves of Future World. These differences play themselves out in the shapes of the hardscape, the stylistic treatment of planters, the plant palette, and the way the plants are maintained. The East side, home to Universe of Energy, Wonders of Life, Mission: SPACE, and Test Track, deals generally with the more technical aspects of modern science. The outdoor spaces are therefore more angular and structured, with hard corners and sculpted plantings. The West side, where we find The Living Seas, The Land, and Journey into Imagination with Figment, covers topics more natural and free-form. This leads to a treatment that is softer and more tactile, with curvilinear edges and lots of water. Even the smooth river rock in the various waterways affect this image because they represent real materials and have the softer shapes the designers required.

The curved pathways and water features of Future World West feel natural.

Plant Life

The planting outside The Land is specifically tied to its purpose. The berms on either side are planted in rows of foliage that embody the natural riches of our land, while the

trees at the top flower in white to indicate clouds. This treatment ends with the tile mosaic at the entrance designed to represent a section cut into the layers of the Earth.

Themed Paving, Epcot Style

Unlike most of the other Disney parks, Epcot's Future World would not benefit from the type of themed paving we apply elsewhere. It would not be appropriate to see flagstone pavers like those of Fantasyland at Magic Kingdom Park or the faux dirt pathways of Harambe at Disney's Animal Kingdom. Instead, we can use the hardscape here to reinforce the thematic emphasis of the Park, as in this small courtyard—seen below—found just beyond the breezeway leading to Future World West. This element, added in 1998 as an enhancement, displays some of the greatest accomplishments in the realms of science, technology, and exploration. This detail adds another layer to the Park's messages.

These paving insets offer an unexpected learning opportunity and reinforce the vision of Future World.

The lush and inviting original exterior of The Land illustrated by Collin Campbell

The Lay of the Land

The Land tells the story of our interaction with this planet and the resources—specifically food—that we take from it in order to survive. This concept is a perfect match with the theories of sustainable living toward a brighter future that underpin much of Future World. At 6 acres, The Land is as big as all of Tomorrowland at the Magic Kingdom—a fitting choice for an attraction with such a grand mission. This scale allows for the inclusion of the large greenhouses seen from the Living with the Land attraction and available walking tours that give the pavilion much of its identity.

The Land was renovated in 2005 to feature a fresh new face representative of current thinking in design relative to nature. The approach to the attraction from the outside was redeveloped to provide a more inviting and naturalistic face for the pavilion. The materials palette was expanded to include natural and rough-cut stone, and a stream was added to cool the space from a sensory standpoint. Inside, the colors are bright and appealing, but inherently natural in feeling, owing to the fact that they are taken from natural elements. There are blues from the sky and greens and earth tones taken from the landscape. The yellow accents are indicative of the sun, which provides so much of the nourishment for all of the wonders of our natural environment. The color palette is taken into a softer range, which ties it all together and avoids an artificial look.

The atrium in the center of the main space is a very intentional device meant to bring real sunlight into the area, unlike almost any other Future World pavilion. This is key to maintaining our sense of connection to the environment even while we're moving about inside a massive structure. The skylight also serves as a reference to the aforementioned greenhouses.

Herb Ryman produced this concept for the desert scene in Living with the Land.

Science Flair

The attraction most central to the themes of The Land is our boat tour of the pavilion, Living with the Land. This ride-through of the greenhouses and accompanying show scenes shows us where we get our food. We are taken first through various climatic zones, such as rain forests and deserts, and told how they differ but together fill their role in the greater ecosystem of the entire planet. We're then told a story about farming—mostly through media, on show sets evocative of the classic American farm. We move from there into the greenhouse to see concepts for the farm of the future, wherever that farm may be. Many of the vegetables served in the Garden Grill Restaurant upstairs are grown here. We learn about hydroponic drip irrigation (a concept put to use in the Rocky Mountains of the Canadian pavilion), soil-free farming in which nutrients are sprayed onto the roots in measured doses, and growth opportunities in difficult settings such as sandy soil and zero-gravity environments in space. This is a component of the Science Department at Epcot. The Park has from its outset maintained a science group that performs real studies at The Land and at The Living Seas, as well as consulting with WDI and Operations on educational programs proposed for any of the Florida parks. A complementary film attraction—*The Circle of Life*—provides an even deeper look into these themes. This update to the original *Symbiosis* makes use of three popular characters from *The Lion King* to make this message accessible to even our youngest Guests.

This inspirational concept by Herb Ryman captures the essence of Living with the Land.

Visual explanation of Soarin' ride system by Ray Spencer

PROFILE OF DOME

Fly Away

The renovation of The Land pavilion in 2005 brought with it an exciting new attraction that made its debut at Disney's California Adventure in 2001. This show, Soarin', takes us on an amazing journey over this great, big, wonderful land of ours. Specifically, California, as this attraction is presented initially as a gift from the California park.

Soarin' can be seen as a spiritual successor to one of the favorite elements from the early days of Epcot—the OmniMax scene from Horizons. Imagineers never forgot how well that effect worked, so we were always looking for a way to make use of it again and to plus the idea even further. During the initial development of the Soarin' concept, Imagineers sought the means to take our Guests on a hang glider, with all the sense of wonder and freedom that that implies. This device allows us to fly our Guests over vistas they could never see without this attraction.

The result of that search is Soarin'. The effect of immersion is heightened by the inclusion of additional sensory inputs such as the smell of a pine forest and the feel of the wind blowing on your face. The seats move gently to indicate changes in your direction of flight, and the theater itself is enhanced to project the audience as fully into the scene as possible. The silent mechanism, developed specifically for this show by WDI engineers, is a marvel of simplicity and unobtrusive operation. Take note of how smoothly and quietly you're moved into position when the lights go down. The engineering effort required to achieve this seamless result is important to our staging of the show. It avoids the outside sensory interference that can pull an audience out of the show.

These conceptual images by Ray Spencer demonstrate the concept of how the attraction functions. When we develop these new ideas, we have to communicate them in a way that allows the viewer to see clearly how this new thing will work. Part of the challenge for the concept designer is to choose the point of view and determine which elements to include that will make this communication clearly readable.

Imagineers Never Stop Playing with Their Toys

When the Soarin' team was searching for possibilities of how to convey the sense of flight to large audiences with an acceptable capacity, ride engineer Mark Sumner turned to his toy box. He brought his 40-year-old erector set down from the attic and started "playing." After a weekend spent sketching and tinkering, he had a model of a new ride mechanism to show to the team. The simple piece, operated by a hand crank and demonstrating an action remarkably similar to the eventual attraction, spurred on a new direction in thinking and a significant R&D effort to turn this toy into a reality.

Imagineer Mark Sumner shows off his weekend project.

Found Nemo!

This photo op in front of The Living Seas was added in 2004 to announce the changes to the attraction, now featuring the great characters from *Finding Nemo*. This provides a setup for the story line, and adds visual interest in the area. It's also a pleasant distraction for children who are in-between attractions. Due to its simple but effective layout, Future World doesn't have as many little off-the-beaten-path destinations as World Showcase or some of the other Disney parks, but we still look for opportunities to add a little detail whenever possible.

Sonic Support

While in Future World, pay attention to the background music. It's different than what you might hear at Magic Kingdom Park or at Disney's Animal Kingdom, right? It's less about a specific time or place and more about a mood and the ideas being explored here. It's chosen by our media designers to reflect the soaring themes and concepts featured in Future World. It can't be pinned to a particular setting or genre, but completes the effect. You might not even notice that it's there as you make your way around, but you miss it if it's not. As Imagineers, we often find ourselves walking through the parks prior to opening, and the absence of the background music is truly striking.

What Goes Up...

This fountain, found outside Journey into Imagination with Figment, surprises us and tries to fool one of our senses by flowing up rather than down. This fits nicely with the new story of Journey into Imagination with Figment, where our senses are put to the test. A place dedicated to the exploration of our imaginations should always be full of surprises.

Go with the Flow

These leapfrog fountains, a favorite of children since the Park's opening, are based on a WDI-developed technology called "laminar flow." This technique, in which the water pressure and the direction of the tubing is very carefully calibrated, creates spurts of water that can "jump" and "hop" and stay together as they fly through the air. By carefully timing the release of the next spurt, we can create the illusion that a single splash of water is hopping from pad to pad. This technology has been installed for effects and interactives in attractions such as Splash Mountain and in area development effects at Disney's Animal Kingdom.

69

Journey into Imagination with Figment

Figment and Dreamfinder, from the original Journey into Imagination, as shown in this concept sketch by Andy Gaskill

The Return of an Old Friend

Everybody changes their mind—even the Imagineers. When the time came (in 1999) to redesign the beloved Journey into Imagination attraction that had opened in 1983, the Company clearly underestimated the level of attachment our Guests felt toward its little purple star, Figment. This dragon was conceived by Tony Baxter upon his realization that no one had ever *identified* the much-talked-of "figment of the imagination."

When Figment was reintroduced during a 2002 renovation, the story possibilities offered up by this character were easy to sense. That is, Figment provided a comedic foil to the stuffy, staid Imagination Institute that had been brought over to the ride as an extension of the back story of the attached *Honey, I Shrunk the Audience* film. His counterpoint to the presentation of Dr. Nigel Channing regarding the impact of the five senses on our imagination—combined with an expanded version of the Sherman brothers' classic song, "One Little Spark"—brought back a bit of the whimsy for which this little corner of Future World had always been known. Figment's friend, Dreamfinder, didn't make the return trip, but does enjoy a respectful homage in the new ride.

Finale scene composite image by Laurie Newell and Alex Wright

QUICK TAKES

• Take note of the names on the office doors here at the Imagination Institute. You'll see one labeled Dean Finder, a not-so-subtle reference to the venerable Dreamfinder from the original attraction.

• The red and white letterman's jacket with the *M* hanging outside the entrance to the computer lab is a reference to Medfield College, the fictional setting of such classic Disney films as *The Absent-Minded Professor* and *The Computer Wore Tennis Shoes*. This also explains the high-top sneakers placed by the door.

• The sheet music being used by Figment as a hang glider in the finale scene includes a few bars of the attraction's theme song, "One Little Spark." The sheet is decorated with a motif paying homage to the Dreamcatcher from Journey into Imagination.

Dreamcatcher silhouette
by Alex Wright

• In the Sight Lab, look for the poster showing the classic optical illusion in which one can see either a goblet or two faces, depending on how one chooses to look. Ours is a specially Imagineered Figment version.

Figment concept sketch
by Larry Nikolai

Once upon a time

Character design development
by Alex Wright

Honey, I Shrunk the Audience

The in-your-face action of Honey, I Shrunk the Audience

In Order to Think Small You've Got to Think Big

How do you make a film more involving? By involving the audience in the film. When the action on-screen makes its way out into the theater, the viewer becomes engaged and will react in a way that no film alone can elicit. *Honey, I Shrunk the Audience* is an important step in our development of these immersive effects. It was the first to make use of large-scale mechanical effects—used to achieve the shaking of the room and the rumbling of the floor as we shrink to our supposed size—as well as effects built into the seat frames such as dog sneezes and mouse tails.

Making Places

Honey, I Shrunk the Audience is also a good place to talk about place making. This is a prime function of WDI's designs, and a big reason that our shows are successful. Place making involves crafting a setting of time and place that will provide the appropriate backdrop to our shows. For this show, an entity—the Imagination Institute—was created as the host of the "Inventor of the Year" awards. This provides the backstory that brings us into the theater and the characters (and the relationships between characters) that will move the story forward. Had we simply dropped in the characters from the *Honey, I Shrunk the Kids* films, the show would have had no context to connect it to the rest of the Park.

3-D Times Three ...

Magic Journeys 1982–1986	*Captain EO* 1986–1994	*Honey, I Shrunk the Audience* 1994–????

Research and Development

Imagineers at work in the R&D Labs

And you thought the rest of us had a lot of fun at work! Well, you were right, but the Imagineers who work in WDI's Research and Development (R&D) division get to do all of the *really* cool stuff. They look for or invent ways to use technologies developed throughout all of industry, from any field imaginable, seperately or in combination, in order to better tell our stories. Walt was always a big proponent of technology, and was insistent that his company never stop searching for new materials and processes. At the Studio, he was known to scrap completed work if a new enhancement had come along that he felt could make the project better. He pushed his crew toward the development of the multiplane camera and other optical processes in the interest of improving the believability of the image.

Today's R&D department leads our exploration in this field, and renders services for many divisions of The Walt Disney Company. They have assisted in the implementation of Enhanced Television components for the ABC Television Network and ESPN Motion for our sports network's Web site, as well as all of the new marvels they provide for our theme parks every day. Recent efforts in that area include Lucky the Dinosaur, an air-launch system for fireworks, our 4-D project scheduling and planning software, and the floating crystal ball for Madame Leota in The Haunted Mansion at Disneyland.

Their work is a combination of purely exploratory efforts—whereby they seek interesting options to bring back to the rest of the group in order to find out if there is an application—and development based on requests from other departments who need some thought put toward solving a particular creative or engineering challenge that they find themselves up against.

WORLD SHOWCASE

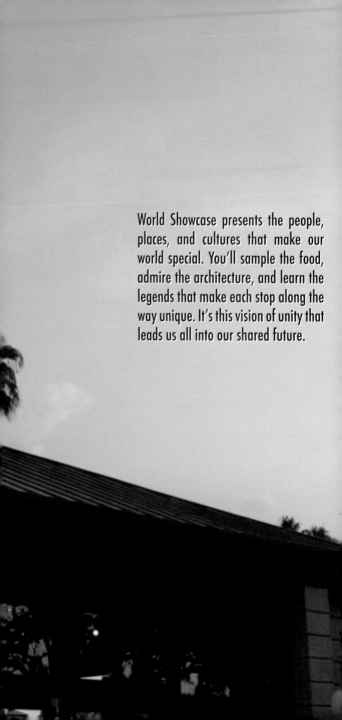

World Showcase presents the people, places, and cultures that make our world special. You'll sample the food, admire the architecture, and learn the legends that make each stop along the way unique. It's this vision of unity that leads us all into our shared future.

Early inspirational illustration by Herb Ryman

Globe-trotting

There was a heartfelt belief held by Walt and his team of Imagineers, who would go on to carry out his dreams for Epcot, that the more people know about one another—our differences and our similarities—the more mutual appreciation we will have of each other and the better we will be able to get along in the pursuit of our shared future. With that in mind, World Showcase was planned as a place where nations and people from around the world would gather to interact with each other, to learn about one another, and to build a common language of experiences. World Showcase takes its cue—as does Future World—from the ambitious visions of the early World's Fairs, which featured participation from nations and commercial enterprises from around the world toward this same goal.

World Showcase did go through several design revisions over the years, right along with the rest of the Park. It went through various notions of staging, many of which bore little resemblance to the finished space. In fact, at one point the entire showcase was to be housed in a series of bays—like slices of a pie—around a central courtyard, very sleek and modernist in appearance. Under this scheme, each nation would be granted equal frontage of identical appearance, and the heavily themed elements would have been withheld for the interior. The spaces would vary in size behind these facades, with deeper slices of pie for certain countries, based on show requirements or sponsor demands.

Study sketch for an early iteration of an international plaza by Herb Ryman

Timeline

World Showcase represents various aspects of the countries presented, including their modern-day identities, but the exterior architecture uses a very specific stylistic attitude as a unifying factor. Besides choosing iconic landmarks that are instantly recognizable in the "long shot," we also limit ourselves to national vernacular building facades in the accompanying streetscapes. This is done to ensure that each country's face portrays a very singular appearance that cannot be mistaken for any other.

This choice derives from our assessment of changes in the direction of world architecture over the course of the latter half of the 20th century. The postwar years saw the appearance of the first regularly scheduled commercial transatlantic flights. This—in addition to rapid increases in communications technologies and an increasingly global economy and cultural base—led to a certain homogenization of architecture and design. There is still plenty of distinctive architecture being done all around the world, but during this time period it became increasingly difficult to identify individual national styles of architecture based on clear and unique design cues.

These time-based guidelines allow us to stick to another of our design goals—that of evoking the emotion and the sense one gets from a place rather than building exact replicas. This dates to the roots of Imagineering in the arts of filmmaking, wherein iconic imagery is favored for the emotional response it elicits.

Early World Showcase concept by Dorothea Redmond demonstrating a varied skyline

Past Time

Promenade view of Mexico by Richard Gutierrez

In attempting to capture the spirit of the Mexican people, Imagineers turned their attention to the origins of that spirit. The resulting pavilion is derived from elements of each of their major pre-Colombian civilizations—the Mayan, the Toltec, and the Aztec—as well as from the Spanish influence that has shaped their architecture and design.

The pyramid you enter to visit Mexico is a composite of Mesoamerican motifs dating back to the 3rd century, emphasizing the Aztec style. Once inside, you find yourself in a gallery showcasing Mexican arts and crafts. The Sun Stone—or Aztec calendar—marks the way to the Plaza de los Amigos (Plaza of the Friends), an open-air marketplace brimming with activity. This market and the adjoining restaurant are placed in a nighttime setting in order to be more authentic to the operating hours of a typical Mexican market. The Spanish-tinged Cantina de San Angel is based on the San Angel Inn of 1692.

Bird's-eye view of Mexico by Tom Gilleon

You're the Expert

Imagineers don't pretend to be the authority on many of the areas of study upon which we focus our designs, so we regularly consult with people who are experts. In World Showcase particularly, it's critical that each pavilion be designed with a real awareness of the cultures being represented. To that end, the team for each location worked with a group of consultants and historians who were able to point out any missteps and make suggestions as to how they might be corrected. In the case of Mexico, our original designs leaned too heavily on the Spanish colonial influence, to the detriment of its rich and valuable ancient cultures. When this was pointed out by a group of foreign exchange students and the Ambassador to Mexico, the team changed the focus of the design significantly.

Plaza-entry concept by Herb Ryman

The festive atmosphere of our Mexico is clearly on display in this distinctive Herb Ryman concept for the seating area at the restaurant.

79

Concept by Tom Gilleon for the approach to the temple entrance

The River of Time

Mexico is a very large country, with a rich and diverse geography and culture. Wrapping that story up into a single attraction is a daunting challenge offering exciting possibilities for scenic, character, and media treatments. It was very important the three cultures of ancient Mexico be represented along the way. We begin the ride on a moonlit river flowing through a central Mexican jungle–an experience very much akin to the introductory scene of Pirates of the Caribbean at Disneyland. This river leads us through a temple entrance, and the show is on. Our boats encounter a series of projections and special effects with scenic murals paying homage to those ancient cultures. These images tell the story, through dance, of the struggle between good and evil as played out between Quetzalcóatl–the feathered serpent–and Tezcatlipoca–the tiger. In order to tell the next part of Mexico's story–the Spanish colonial era–Imagineers took inspiration from another of their classic attractions–"it's a small world." The Día de los Muertos scene in particular–based on the Mexican "Day of the Dead" festival celebrating the lives and memories of the deceased–draws heavily on its scenic arrangement, the tone of the music, the design of the childlike characters, and the simple, charming animation. This version has its own

Elevation of scenic flats by Eddie Martinez

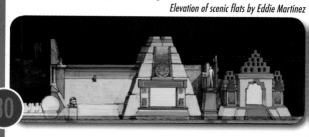

THE DANCE OF THE TIGER

Character design sketches by X. Atencio

spin, however. All of the dolls and set pieces in this scene are represented as papier-mâché, with confetti fringe and very bright colors reminiscent of piñatas. The next segment brings us forward to modern-day Mexico, with its vibrant marketplace, striking coastline, and many popular tourist destinations. We then make our way into the finale, which features a celebration taking place on a replica of Mexico City's Reforma Boulevard, with singing, dancing, and fireworks. Throughout the attraction, music is a vital element of the show. This is a nod to a Mayan myth that holds that the gods granted the gift of song to the Earth, and that "Life was all music from that time on." The songs and audio track bring this attraction to life with an energy that keeps you humming along on your way out the door and on to your next adventure.

Concept sketch by Ray Aragon of the character Quetzalcóatl preparing for battle with Tezcatlipoca. This sequence—seen on multiple screens as one passes through—is storyboarded just like a film.

A view down a Mexican street as rendered by Tom Gilleon. This concept captures the charm and the inviting image that the design team hoped to create throughout the attraction.

81

The view from the San Angel Inn, illustrated by Tom Gilleon

I Sea, I Sea

Overall concept of Norway by Collin Campbell

When approaching the design process for each country in World Showcase, we look for a central idea that will capture the country's unique spirit. In the case of Norway, the obvious starting point is that nation's seafaring heritage. The Norwegian people are connected to the sea and to their natural environment in a way that permeates their designs.

Our showcase pavilion for Norway is a charming little cobblestone plaza, reminiscent of those found in the coastal cities of Bergen, Alesund, Oslo, and the Setesdal Valley. These maritime locales, hewn from natural materials with superb craftsmanship, evoke the character of the Norwegian people and their connection to the sea. This bond is evidenced by the Viking Ship play area that was added to the pavilion in 1998 and is modeled after Dragon-headed 10th-century Norse explorer ships, much like the ones Guests board to make their journey into the Maelstrom. This notion is carried further by the waterfall that makes its way out of that attraction and toward our town center. The 14th-century Norwegian castle Akershus—which overlooks the harbor in Oslo—inspired the design of the restaurant and carries on the seaside theme.

Material Facts

The finishes and materials chosen to represent the architecture of Norway are critical to establishing its visual authenticity. We put our Character Plaster and Character Paint departments to the test in replicating the aged stone, stucco, rockwork, and wood surfaces that embody the relationship of the Norwegian people to their natural environment. The characteristic rosemaling details painted onto the wood surfaces by our scenic artisans complete the look and add that last little layer of authenticity to finish off the scene.

Two paint elevations of Norway facades by Katie Olson show character-paint intent. These illustrations serve as a guide to the painters working in the field.

Stave Church

The prominence of the Stave Church—or *Stavkirke*—in our pavilion is no accident. These churches, once found throughout the country in almost every little town and village, were key components to the village center. At one point in time there were over 1,000 in Norway, but today they number only twenty-eight, as many were thought to have been replaced during the Middle Ages as "obsolete." Those that remain are some of the oldest wooden structures currently in existence.

This color elevation by Katie Olson illustrates the quality of the wood and the level of aging and distressing desired by the designers as the Stave Church was finished in the field. The finished structure shows exactly that character.

Maelstrom

Concept for the top of the drop by Sam McKim

Troll On!

Looking at the world as Imagineers do, through the eyes of storytellers, we often find that the best way to learn about a group of people is by studying the stories they tell one another. The folklore and mythology of a culture can be a very telling indicator regarding the values and interests of the people of that culture. Maelstrom takes these stories, using them as a mechanism to send us on a trip through time, so that we might contrast the history and modern-day reality of the country of Norway.

We start with imagery of old Norse mythology, with Odin beckoning you to partake in this adventure. This sets the stage for our excursion into the wild forest of Norway. Norwegians are rightfully proud of their natural environments, so this is a recurring theme throughout the boat ride and the subsequent film. Here we are confronted by a three-headed troll, common in Norwegian folk tales, protective of the forest. The backward drop—a unique feature at the time of its debut—is the real plunge into the diverse locales and periods of history that give Norway its character.

At the departure point, in a typical Norwegian coastal village of today, we make our way in to see a film that further explores the places and the people that make Norway what it is today. This film was directed by Paul Gerber—who also directed *Symbiosis* and *The Seas* for Epcot.

Mural for an early study model by Joe Rohde

Exploratory Art

Multiple concepts for Maelstrom by Joe Rohde

Before the development of a finished attraction such as this one can begin in earnest, the design team will explore many different potential directions for the show to take. This series of concepts by Joe Rohde captures the mood and the spirit of what the design team hoped to achieve with Maelstrom. The colors set the atmosphere, and the imagery begins to put forth the variety of subject matter that would need to be included to adequately present this nation. Some of these exploratory sketches will find their way to the finished show, but many will not.

Great Walls of China

Inspirational concept by Herb Ryman

Our presentation for China takes its cues primarily from the architecture of ancient China, focusing on the Imperial Palace (or Forbidden City) and the Temple of Heaven park. These two locations are found on opposite ends of the city, much the same as the manner in which they are presented here. We enter the showcase by passing through the Zhao Yang Men, which translates as "Gate of the Golden Sun." This gate was modeled after the one at the emperor's summer palace near Beijing. The dominant element in the skyline of our China is the Hall of Prayer for Good Harvest. This striking tower is an imperial prayer temple, where the emperor would go to pray for a good harvest or give thanks for one that had already passed.

This agricultural theme pervades the detailing of the hall's interior. Note the four columns in the center, each representing one of the seasons of the year. The twelve exterior columns are indicative of the twelve months of the year and of the twelve year cycle that the Chinese live by. In Chinese design, circles define the heavens and squares stand in for the earth—used together they form the universe. This motif repeats itself throughout the building. The red and yellow that are found all around represent happiness and the emperor, respectively. The original hall was built solely with interlocking pieces of wood—no nails or fasteners.

Don't Forget to Look Up

The medallion inset into the top of the prayer hall is an important symbol for the building and is representative of the Chinese culture. The dragon and the phoenix each carry meaning—the dragon is indicative of power (and if it has five claws, it specifically refers to the power of the emperor), and the phoenix represents peace and prosperity. Together they signify a marriage.

QUICK TAKES

Decorative figures on rooftops have specific meanings.

• The man seated on the hen on the roof of Nine Dragons Restaurant is Prince Min, a 3rd-century ruler who was hanged for his cruelty. It is customary to install an effigy of him as a warning to other tyrants. The various animals are placed there to keep him from escaping.

• Xing Fu Jie, or "Street of Good Fortune," serves as the exit corridor for *Reflections of China*. It was intentionally designed to be too small for the number of Guests exiting the show in order to re-create the sense of crowding one feels on the streets of China.

87

Development concept by Tom Gilleon

Roundabout

In our attempt to capture the beauty and scope of a country the size of China, we turned to a favorite device capable of capturing the imagery we wanted to see—our trusty Circle-Vision 360 camera rig. This marvel, originally developed for Disneyland where it initially presented *America the Beautiful*, envelops an audience fully into a scene in a way that is unique in the realm of film and projection technologies.

After catching a presentation at the Cinerama theater in Hollywood, Walt had the idea for Circle-Vision and set some of his best studio craftsmen on the task. He didn't see any reason that the three screens of Cinerama couldn't be expanded to a full circle. The original development of Circle-Vision was fraught with trial and error, as the development team struggled to pin down just the right number of cameras (nine) and the best means of moving this 600-pound rig around the countryside—while staying out of the shot and maintaining good sight lines all the way around. They shot miles of film and saw much of the local scenery along the way.

Reflections of China is an update to the film *Wonders of China* that played at Epcot from 1982 through 2003. *Wonders of China* represented the first time that a film crew from the West was allowed access to film inside the country's borders in many years. The Disney crew worked closely with an assigned Chinese crew to capture the footage. This was the first time many sights, such as the Forbidden City, the Summer Palace, and the Leshan Buddha, had been seen on film by Western audiences.

The host for our journey—then and now—is the poet Li Bai, from the 8th century, during the Tang Dynasty. He is considered to be the poet immortal of Chinese literature, and left a body of work numbering 1,100 poems. He is an appropriate choice for such an assignment, as he is known to have traveled extensively throughout China for much of his life, as his wealth and fame enabled him to do.

One of the advantages of filmed presentations in World Showcase is that they offer us the opportunity for updates in order to keep up with changes that occur over time in the countries. In the case of China, great cultural advancements had occurred making it necessary to revitalize the film so as to remain true to the realities of China today. While much of the central structure was kept, including the guidance of Li Bai, many scenes of present-day Hong Kong, Macau, and Shanghai were added into the mix. The lyrical beauty of the provinces and the grand variety of geography found across China are given a vibrant counterpoint through the inclusion of these modern marvels and world-class cities.

On set in China with Theme Park Productions

A Theme Park Productions Production

Almost all of the media found in Disney parks is produced by Theme Park Productions, Inc. (TPP), a sister company to WDI. This list would include animated segments such as the film from *Mickey's PhilharMagic* at Magic Kingdom Park; live-action footage supporting our stories, as in Timekeeper in Tomorrowland; as well as sweeping documentaries that capture the grandeur of a particular place for one of our World Showcase presentations.

TPP is also responsible for the generation of many of our on-screen interactive media components for some of our custom games, our attraction post-shows, and our Innoventions exhibits.

TPP is a specialized group made up of directors, producers, editors, media designers, and others, who function much like a stand-alone production house one might find in Hollywood. They go through the same sort of process as well, while adding the Disney brand of storytelling to their work. They write scripts, draw storyboards, scout locations, schedule shoots, and audition and hire on-screen performers and vocal talent.

Having this group as a resource for the production of our attractions is a luxury for the Creative department within WDI, as TPP is much more in tune with the unique nature of our development process than any Hollywood production house would be. This allows for the continual plussing of our ideas that we like to engage in at all steps of the process right through opening day.

The German pavilion at dusk rendered by Bob Scifo

Geschichte Means "Story"

The center of any prototypical Bavarian village is the *platz*, or plaza—the equivalent of an American town square. This classic image of German townships, replete with architectural styles ranging from the 13th to the 17th centuries, gives our Germany the instant recognition that is required of our designs in the World Showcase. Again, we fall back on a design approach calling for the iconic image rather than a completist attempt to include elements from the entire country in one small pavilion.

Our buildings are drawn from sources throughout the region. The castle walls at the rear are a combination of Eltz Castle near Koblenz and Stahleck Fortress on the Rhine near Bacharach. The exterior of the Biergarten is clearly inspired by the one in Rothenburg ob der Tauber. The smaller facades in the village are taken from places such as the Römerburg Platz in Frankfurt, Freiburg, and Rothenburg once again. In most cases, one would not see a direct translation of the original buildings in the ones we present. One of the skills of our style of design is the careful selection of reference material—from the big-picture image to the smallest details—and the ability to recombine them into new pieces that fit with our story intent. This is one of the legacies within our art derived from the techniques of motion-picture art direction, where even a period piece becomes a pastiche of elements woven into a backdrop that is more evocative than literal.

The Biergarten itself is a loving homage to the idyllic festival settings in our romanticized notions of Germany. It's placed in an exterior nighttime setting to allow for warm lights and the glow of the tree canopy. The character finishes in this courtyard recall so many of the classic Disney fairy tales. This is a more theatrical treatment than that of the exterior spaces. These elements conspire to create an atmosphere of friendship and frivolity.

We Don't Have Room for Everyone

The Gild Hall, a 16th-century merchants hall, is inspired by the Kaufhaus in Freiburg. The original, however, has four figures on its face rather than our three. In order to fit the scale of our village, we had to eliminate one of the original's four Hapsburg emperors. Maximilian I failed to make the trip to Epcot—leaving Philip I, Charles V, and Ferdinand I to represent this European royal family that ruled Austria-Hungary from 1273–1918.

Color elevation of Bavarian village haus by Julie Svendsen

Dragon Slayer

The statue in the courtyard is of St. George slaying a dragon. St. George is the patron saint of soldiers. German legends say that St. George killed a dragon to which a king's daughter was being sacrificed—slaying it with his magical sword, Ascalon. Almost all German villages have a statue of St. George as a symbol of protection. Ours is modeled after the one in Rothenburg.

Concept sketch of Italy by Herb Ryman

Now, *That's* Italian!

Our Italy pavilion is weighted toward the architecture of Venice. It's not the most representative architectural style for the entire country, but is the most distinctive and perhaps the most recognizable as being Italian. Our departure point is the Piazza di San Marco, or St. Mark's Square. The landmark structures are the Doge's Palace, constructed between the 9th and the 16th centuries—spanning Gothic and Renaissance styles—and the Campanile clock-bell tower built one-fifth the size of the original.

The two columns at the entrance to the piazza mimic those that grace the original. One holds a statue of a lion—the guardian of Venice—and the other shows St. Theodore slaying a dragon. The Arcata d'Artigiani, a stucco building with a clay-tile roof, brings together elements of the rural region of Tuscany. The Fontana di Nettuno is intended to capture the spirit of the work of the prolific Renaissance sculptor, artist, and architect Gian Lorenzo Bernini, but is not based upon any particular piece.

Fountain maquette by George Snowdo

Shop designs come to life in these interior concepts by Dorothea Redmond.

Color elevations by Nicole Armitage Doolittle

Water, Water, Everywhere . . .

In order to further evoke the atmosphere of Venice, the Isola del Lago (Isle of the Lake) was built out onto World Showcase Lagoon. This allows for the inclusion of some characteristic bridges—a necessity, owing to the fact that the city was built on more than 100 islands—and the colorful mooring posts and gondolas that inhabit the signature canals and really set our scene. Spatially, this draws the pavilion across the promenade and offers some great viewing of the lagoon.

This study sketch, by Herb Ryman, presages the canal treatment at the lagoon.

Mirror, Mirror . . .

The plaza overall is presented as a mirror image of the original. This exemplifies WDI's preference for composing a unified design as opposed to simply creating replicas. The height of the Campanile combined with the mass of the Doge's Palace and The American Adventure pavilion created an imbalance in the skyline when placed in their "proper" positions. So, the designers relocated the Doge's Palace to compensate.

Illustration of the plaza by Bob Scifo

93

Herb Ryman's immense talents allowed him to render a scene many different ways...

Adventurous Design

One of the most delicate tasks facing the designers of World Showcase was determining the proper way to present the host nation, the United States. As gracious hosts, the United States could not be seen as an overly dominant presence on the promenade. On the other hand, Disney is a quintessentially American company, and it was important to give America a grandeur befitting its status as hometown favorite.

The result of a great deal of exploration was the choice to place the pavilion directly across from the entrance to World Showcase, giving it a place of prominence and establishing it in the role of host. The decision was also made to design it in the style of a colonial American manor house, in order to evoke the most definitive period in our nation's history. The edifice is intended to portray "America's Mansion," rather than any particular governmental hall, in keeping with the rest of the Showcase.

... as in these two concepts for The American Adventure with vastly different moods.

By George, I Think That's It!

Our building's edifice is an example of English Georgian architecture, prevalent during the 18th-century reigns of King George I through King George IV, and therefore common in colonial America as well. This style expresses itself in the Greek-revivalist porticos, the stone-quoined corners implying strength and solidity, and the characteristic clock and bell tower above the roof. This look carries over to the American Gardens Theater, designed as a fitting complement to the main building.

This detail from a model of an earlier version of Epcot shows The American Adventure in its one-time location atop the entrance to the World Showcase. In the end, however, the pavilion was moved to the far side of the lagoon—still welcoming arriving Guests as they see it across the water, but also serving to ensure that they would make the trip all the way around World Showcase.

Red, White, and Blue All Over

The color palette at The American Adventure is very tightly controlled. One can see in all of the concept art throughout its development that this was always on the minds of the design team. The red, white, and blue color scheme repeats itself throughout the pavilion. We see a red promenade, white pilasters on the marquee, and a blue-tile fountain. We have 110,000 red bricks, white architectural trim, and the blue sky backdrop. The flowers are always planted in red, white, and blue groupings. And there's always a layer of banners and buntings declaring the patriotic leanings of the place.

The American Adventure

Our hosts for this journey through time and history enjoy the view from the Statue of Liber...

Adventures in Theater

The show at The American Adventure is one of Imagineering's most ambitious efforts in the area of multimedia theater. It can be thought of as an extension of the presentation techniques behind Carousel of Progress, in which a variety of visual and auditory devices are used to tell a story of history that traverses significant changes throughout time. Like Carousel—though far more ambitious and advanced—The American Adventure uses a combination of theatrical devices, both complex and simple, to tell one of the most important stories we've ever told.

Whenever possible, that story is told from the perspective of the common man. This change came about during the story development of the show. Originally, the Valley Forge scene featured George Washington delivering an inspirational address to the troops from atop his horse. Despite numerous rewrites, the scene just wasn't working until Imagineer Randy Bright proposed the addition of the two soldiers who deliver the story and lend it weight and impact through their experiences. This approach is seen throughout the rest of the show, as in the Depression-era scene on the porch of the general store and in the World War II shipyard.

These sculptural icons, created by Imagineering sculptors, celebrate the Spirits of Ameri...

The Benjamin Franklin figure from this scene, in which Thomas Jefferson is writing the Declaration of Independence, is a landmark in WDI Audio-Animatronics design. He walks up the steps to enter the scene, and then walks across the room to join Mr. Jefferson in conversation. This requires a great deal of engineering effort, to accommodate the various support, power, and control functions that must service the figure.

QUICK TAKES

• In order to maintain the story integrity, no subject matter predating the invention of the camera is presented in (staged) photography or film. These time periods are shown only in artwork or dimensional scenes using Audio-Animatronics. This is in keeping with a WDI philosophy articulated by Marc Davis stating that we can set up the rules for these worlds that we create any way we please, but once we do set the rules, we must be absolutely consistent in the way we follow them.

• The stage measures 130 feet by 50 feet, roughly one-fourth the size of a football field. The screen is 28 feet by 155 feet—the largest rear-projection screen ever.

• A 65-foot by 35-foot scene changer—weighing 175 tons—moves the show sets into place horizontally. They are then lifted into view by telescoping hydraulic supports—with all the accompanying electrical and hydraulic feeds intact. Seven additional lifts bring sets into view from the sides and from above. Every aspect of the operation is controlled by a network of more than two dozen computers.

Mulitiplane background for the Frederick Douglass scene by Bob Scifo

Forcing the Matter

The scene changes in The American Adventure allow us to move through time and draw the audience's focus around the space just the way we want. Look closely, and you'll note the extensive use of multiplane camera imagery in the background illustrations. This tool derives from Disney's Feature Animation studio, where it has been used to add realism to painted scenes. The dimensional pieces on set move in concert with the projections to further enhance the illusion.

97

A Colorful Theory

The color palette for The American Adventure is established in this concept by Herb Ryman.

Red, White, White, White, White, and Blue

As you make your way around Epcot, you might find yourself making certain assumptions about the colors you see. For example, you might be forgiven for believing at first glance that the white trim you see on the facade of The American Adventure is just...white. You'd be wrong, but there are reasons for you to think that.

The issues of scale we deal with are different from those that are seen in the rest of the world. We exaggerate the size of some of our buildings and alter the span of the hard scape between those buildings in order to maintain the appropriate pedestrian scale and sight lines to our theatrical backdrop. We fill in spaces with complementary details, adding layers of depth to the environment. Because of all of these factors, we need to be careful in our application of color.

John Hench—an Imagineer of the highest order—was largely responsible for refining our philosophies of color and served as the principal designer of Epcot. He had begun his Disney career as an artist with Walt's Feature Animation studio. When he came over to WED Enterprises, he brought an unrivaled eye for color and an acute awareness of the ways colors interact with each other, with their environments, and over varying distances. For Cinderella Castle at Magic Kingdom Park, he specified seven different shades of gray for the stone trim at different elevations. At Epcot, he determined the original color palette for Future World and finessed the details of World Showcase in order to show off each country at its best. For The American Adventure, this means that there are actually four different shades of white used for the trim from the bottom of the building to the top. The variation is subtle but critical. John knew better than anyone that this was actually the way to make all of the white pieces look alike.

White, White, White, White, Why?

There are several reasons for the use of these varying tints. First, we have to understand the properties of the color at hand. White can be a powerful color, but must be dealt with very carefully because it is so highly reflective. A white in a Disney Park is typically not a pure white. White can be found in a broad range of warm or cool tones and in an infinite number of individual values. Imagineers play with a *really* big set of crayons!

The biggest influence on color choice is the ambient light. John found the quality of the light in Florida to be very exciting—and very different from that found at WDI's California home. He wouldn't make final decisions on color selections for major elements being built for Florida without first seeing the color on-site so that the environmental light could be taken into account. The effect of this light on our perception of color is seen on some of the changes that occur toward the upper reaches of the building.

A related factor is the color of the sky. As with the light, the color of blue in any sky varies from place to place—dependent upon the geographical latitude, the proximity to bodies of water which affect humidity, and other environmental factors such as particulates in the air. The striking blue sky of Florida reacts strongly with any white placed in the foreground, so we have to alter the tones at the top of the building accordingly.

The reflectivity of white means that it interacts strongly with other colors. It contrasts sharply with surrounding values and hues. The warm tones of the bricks of the lower facade require a warm white for balance—lest the brick make the white look too cool by nature of the side-by-side comparison. Conversely, the trim on the roof above has to be shifted to a cooler tint in order to work well with the deep, dark blue.

While the details and specific properties will differ, these principles can be applied to any color family. This type of study is entirely separate, as well, from the theories of color that dictate which colors we might choose to combine in order to evoke the moods or emotions we wish to project.

Detail of color elevation for The American Adventure by John Hench

A Moving Moment [Norway]

Maelstrom at Norway offers up a tried-and-true method of activating an exterior space that Imagineers have employed since the early days. The little peek outside that each of the boats makes before the final drop allows passing Guests to see what they're in for, and provides movement in the courtyard. This can be thought of in the same vein as the runoff chute at Splash Mountain at the Magic Kingdom, the garden scene in Alice in Wonderland at Disneyland, and the high-speed loop around the front of the building over at Test Track. This bit of kinetics gives any space life, and serves as a "weenie" to draw Guests into the attractions.

The Romantic Road

FÜSSEN

Isn't it Romantic? [Germany]

The inspiration for our miniature train in Germany comes from the Romantic Road between Füssen and Wurzburg. Once one of the most important trade routes in Europe, it is now a popular tourist destination. This project—a collaboration between WDI, WDW Architecture & Design, Epcot Operations, and Horticulture— celebrates the German affinity for model railroading.

Details, Details, Details [United Kingdom]

Note the chimney stacks on top of the merchandise shops in the United Kingdom. These architectural details are not only correct and varied, but have been given a dusting of faux soot to make them appear broken in.

Signs and Designs [France]

It might be easy to stroll past this kiosk without noticing it or the posted bills. That's exactly the point! We don't take note of it because this sort of detail is such a part of the urban landscape. That's why it's so essential to a re-creation of a place. Ours is specific to a Parisian streetscape, and required extensive design of the kiosk itself and the signs to fill it.

Sound Gardening [Japan]

The traditional water garden found between the pagoda and the Yakitori House displays the unique approach taken by the Japanese in their garden designs. This means a more sculpted, manicured approach that

can often involve motion and sound rather than simply appealing to our senses of sight and smell. These are typically pieces driven by the movement of water or wind, such as chimes or bamboo noisemakers.

101

Forced Perspective

At the Canadian pavilion, we see one of the clearest applications of the theatrical design technique of forced perspective. The Hotel du Canada is representative of the common approach, which is to take an object that cannot be built at full scale without overwhelming its site and environment, and making it appear bigger than it is, or at least fool the eye into thinking it's the appropriate size. This is a perpetual concern in the design of theme parks, which want to evoke certain feelings of comfort and reassurance, and don't have the real estate to devote to massive structures, lest their visitors find themselves worn out by walking around such big building footprints.

For the Hotel du Canada, designers desired to make this facade appear suitably noble and majestic, fitting of the source material upon which it is based. However, they had a three- to four-story building that needed to appear to be six or seven stories. In order to pull off this illusion, several tools would need to be employed.

The first trick that helps to fool the eye is the fact that the building begins atop a landing, several feet above the promenade. This means the Guests are always looking up at the structure the first time they view it, taking away the sense of context for the pedestrian down on the main walk.

Next we see the reduction in scale of the building blocks of the Hotel—in this case the limestone blocks from which it is supposedly constructed. You'll note that the blocks up at the top are significantly smaller in the upper floors than near the bottom, much like the stones of Cinderella Castle at Magic Kingdom Park.

Lastly, we shrink all of the architectural ornamentation that dresses the upper stories and the roof. Those windows are tiny! The moldings and dormers and finials are all about half the size they would be expected to be on a real-world example of this type of building.

Perspective Forced

It's the opposite of forced perspective. Not really, but it's forced perspective put to use to create an effect that is the opposite of what we usually want. When we design our sets, typically the technique of forced perspective is used to make our spaces look larger, our buildings look taller, and our distances look greater. In the case of The American Adventure, however, we had to do exactly the reverse.

Due to the spatial requirements of the enormous show inside the building, our exterior facade had to be much bigger than a building that would have been found in the Colonial American time period that serves as our setting. Structures of that era would generally not exceed two or three stories in height, owing in part to the materials and building technologies available at the time. We found ourselves in the unusual position of having to make the equivalent of a five-story building believable as a two-and-a-half-story-tall manor house.

So, the usual tools are applied in reverse. The windows get relatively larger as we move higher up on the building face. Running above the first-story windows, there is a course of bricks falsely implying a story break. The architectural details at the roof level are oversize, at least when compared to the features on a period-correct Colonial building. Imagineer John Hench added another piece to the illustration when he insisted that there be a row of boxwood hedges placed along the base of the building wherever possible, so that it would be difficult for the viewer to truly see the point at which the building meets the ground. This removes the context that would allow a Guest to better realize just how tall each of those floors would be.

Overall concept of the Japan pavilion by Tom Gilleon

Balancing Act

In order to evoke the serenity and drama of traditional Japanese settings, WDI designers drew heavily upon the underlying principles of Japanese design. Among these are balance, harmony, simplicity, formality, and delicacy. The pavilion is laid out in such a way as to place all of the major elements within view of the central entry point, from the symbolic gate on the lagoon to the massive walls of the feudal palace to the soaring majesty of the protective pagoda. The arrangement of all of these elements serves to tie the space together and connect the viewer to his or her surroundings.

Choices were made in the selection of references in order to maintain that distinctly Japanese sensibility. For instance, the original design of the pagoda was deemed by our Japanese advisors to reflect more of the Chinese influence, dating to the time before the Japanese had adapted their pagoda designs to suit their own preferences. So, it was changed.

The detail demonstrated in this color elevation by Tim Braniff allows us to achieve the proper end result, as with the torii gate on the waterfront in Japan.

We Did Our Homework

Japan features perhaps more specific re-creations of real buildings than any of our other pavilions. Making the rounds, we see the following landmarks serving as our reference points.

Paint elevation for Goju-no-to by Tim Braniff

• The red torii gate in the lagoon is based on the one that serves as the entrance to the Itsukushima Shrine on the Inland Sea. Torii are found throughout Japan. Originally conceived as perches for roosters to welcome the new day, they have come to symbolize good luck and purification.

• The pagoda is drawn after one at the 8th-century Horyuji Temple in Nara. Each story represents one of the five elements of the Buddhist universe, in ascending order—Earth, Water, Fire, Wind, and Heaven.

• Yakitori House is representative of the tea house at the Katsura Imperial Villa, commissioned by the ruler Hideyoshi, and designed by an architect who gave three conditions before he would take the job—no limits on expense, no limits on time available for completion, and no interference from the patron until the job was done. WDI designers have been trying to make these demands ever since...to no avail.

• The fortress in the back is taken from Shirasagi-Jo, a 17th-century castle overlooking Hemeji, used by regional kings during the feudal era.

The legs at the base of the torii gate are covered with barnacles. These faux crustaceans imply age and exposure to the elements. Our scenic treatments take into account the relatively obvious influences, such as sun, water, wind, and general damage, in addition to site-specific elements such as barnacles growing on a centuries-old man-made structure in the water.

American Heritage Gallery concept by Chris Turner

Dedication to the Arts

World Showcase has the greatest concentration of gallery spaces in any of the Disney parks. These galleries are important parts of our attempts to tell the story of people from around the world—through art, artifacts, pop culture, and treasured cultural symbols. The galleries of World Showcase are worth the trip all on their own.

The Collections Management group within WDI is responsible for maintaining our displays and the articles that make up the gallery shows. They adhere to the strictest standards of display protocol and work to maintain relationships with institutions, governments, and private lenders that allow us to continue to present first-rate installations. In this side of the business, your reputation is everything.

This adherence has allowed us to present some truly remarkable exhibits over the course of Epcot's existence. Our Imperial China display was seen here for the first time outside Chinese borders. The Disney-Tishman collection installed in The American Heritage Gallery is an important body of African and African American art. Our Japanese Tin Toy exhibit was loaned to us by a generous Japanese collector because of his trust in our protocols.

Those standards come into play with our facility designs, our casework designs, and our lighting and mechanical designs. They cover environmental concerns—such as preventing water intrusion and dust accumulation. They involve proper handling of artifacts—the white glove treatment, and all that. They protect articles from exposure—lighting is limited to a specified level of foot-candles depending upon the material. Anything that could compromise the archival integrity of an item, its aesthetics, or its life span is taken into account.

Gallery images from around World Showcase

The Art of the Story

It is imperative to us that any exhibit installed in a World Showcase gallery tell a story. It might be about an important period in the history of a country. It might be a journey taken by a people centuries ago. It might tell us something we don't know about a particularly vibrant time in a country's history. Our curatorial focus is definitely on finding a story around which to build an exhibit. This is not a practice unique to Disney, but it is one we hold particularly valuable, and from which we never waver. Combining these two elements so central to our nature enables us to create experiences for our Guests that add layers of richness to the World Showcase.

Norway gallery concept by Chris Turner

This concept by Dorothea Redmond captures the intrigue of Morocco.

Morocco

Added in 1984, our Moroccan pavilion brought a new continent to the World Showcase. This attraction offers some of the most exquisite architectural detailing ever put into a Disney park. In order to ensure the authenticity of the presentation, King Hassan II of Morocco sent some of his finest craftsmen, or *maalems*, to work on site with the Imagineers to generate the hundreds of thousands of square feet of carved stone and tile work required to give the place the appropriate finish.

Our Morocco takes inspiration from the cities of Casablanca, Marrakesh, Rabat, and Fez. It is drawn from the traditions of Islamic architecture. The pavilion, like most Moroccan cities, is divided into two sections—the *ville nouvelle*, or new city, and the Medina, or old city.

The gateway to the city—the Bab Boujouloud Gate from Fez—defines the entrance to the Medina. Such gates were typically part of the protective system of the old cities, and were therefore not very welcoming. Ours has been tweaked and given a more pleasant context so that it will work better for our purposes.

The Nejjarine Fountain to the right of the restaurant is also from Fez, and is representative of most of the villages in Morocco.

The minarets, or prayer towers, that form our Moroccan skyline are replicas of the Chella minaret from the capital city of Rabat and the Koutoubia minaret from Marrakesh.

The Layered Look Is In

The layering of spaces shown in this image is quite typical of the way we design our parks. It is particularly applicable here in Morocco, where it implies the continuation of the marketplace beyond what we can see. We tend to want our spaces in the parks to appear larger than they actually are, so we make use of this scenic device to impart a sense of scale. It offers a variety of focal points, and leads your eye on a tour as it picks up details one by one at varying distances from your point of view. Note the framing of the themed lighting fixture, the middle-ground archway leading you in, and the silhouette of the tower all the way in the back to give it focus.

Morocco courtyard concept by Herb Ryman

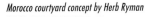

The view toward the France pavilion envisioned by Tom Gilleon

La Belle France

The France pavilion derives most of its look from the beautiful city of Paris. Not just any part of Paris, but specifically those elements dating from La Belle Epoque, or Beautiful Age—the period between 1850 and 1900, during which Baron Von Haussmann ruled the master planning of the city and imparted an aesthetic that today makes Paris one of the most striking and beautiful cities in the world. This was known as the Grand Design, which specified the elegant mansard roofs and dormers that are so characteristically Parisian. Buildings were limited to seven stories, creating a comfortable pedestrian environment.

Designers were sure to capture the essence of a visit to France, with details such as the sidewalk cafe, the prevalence of water fountains, the arcade entrances, and the provincial France depicted on Le Petit Rue—the little street at the rear of the pavilion. The Eiffel Tower, of course, provides us with perhaps the most distinctive signature of any city in the world.

Exterior building elevation by Gordon Hoopes

Tag Team

These two concept images by two different WDI artists show one way our projects can progress through the production pipeline. In this case, the pencil sketch by the art director is handed

Art-direction sketch by Harry Webster

off to a concept designer for further development. The art director has established the overall look and atmosphere, so the concept designer adds more detail, color, and visual clarity for the rest of the design disciplines to follow.

Concept sketch by Tom Gilleon

QUICK TAKES

• The park bordering the canal overlooking the International Gateway is inspired by *A Sunday Afternoon on the Island of La Grande Jatte*, by the post-Impressionist painter Georges Seurat.

• The costumes of the female Cast Members at *Impressions de France* are taken from the painting *A Bar at the Folies-Bergère*, the last major work by the painter Edouard Manet. The colors and a bit of the trim have been changed, but the cut is practically a direct lift.

• The bridge into France from the United Kingdom is a replica of the original Pont des Arts, a pedestrian bridge across the Seine, which was torn down and replaced in 1970.

• Our Eiffel Tower was constructed using the blueprints originally drawn by Gustave Eiffel—only at one-tenth the size.

• The mansarded roof—with two slopes on each of the four sides, the lower slope steeper than the upper—takes its name from the architect Francois Mansard, who worked in Paris in the mid-1600s.

111

Impressions de France

Entry lobby for Impressions de France

First *Impressions*

As we enter the Palais du Cinema, inspired by the palatial Château de Fontainebleau, we are immediately struck by the sheer enchantment this attraction presents. From the ornately patterned decor to the lilting background music to the costumes on the French Cast Members who welcome us to the theater, the ambience is decidedly elegant. It's only fitting when your subject matter is the beautiful country of France.

Our presentation takes place in a 350-seat theater with a 200-degree panoramic view provided by a series of five twenty-seven-and-a-half-feet wide by twenty-one-feet-tall screens. The effect is more subtle than that of Circle-Vision, but equally engrossing and more suited to a focused tour with a narrative thread. Our journey becomes a guided tour in sight and sound through the French countryside, the city streets, the natural wonders, and the landmark buildings.

The rich legacy of classical music for which France is renowned is our launching point. When combined with the symphonic score—a compendium of selections by French composers such as Debussy, Saint-Saëns, and Ravel—the images place us right in the heart of the French locales depicted on-screen. The effect is poetic, inspiring, enticing, and entirely befitting the subject matter.

As with all of our World Showcase films, we hope to show not just the beauty of the architecture, the vastness of the landscape, or the depth of the history—but the warmth of the people and the manner in which they live. This is central to Epcot's mission, and serves to bring the viewer a more personal connection to a faraway land. In the case of France, this intent is served by the scenes of the provincial marketplace, the skiers navigating the French Alps, the folks strolling the banks of the Seine, and the families gathered for a wedding ceremony in one of the most picturesque settings imaginable.

Inspirational sketch of Italy by Dorothea Redmond

Speaking of Film...

It's no mistake that some of the earliest conceptual work done for World Showcase—particularly when the overall design direction was being explored—was performed by landmark Imagineers Herb Ryman and Dorothea Redmond. These two brought with them extensive experience working as art directors in the motion picture industry. Each of them had a knack for capturing a time, place, and mood in a single image in a way that is instantly recognizable. This is done all the time in design for film, and it's a skill Walt wanted to bring to his new medium of the theme park. It is clearly the design approach taken with World Showcase. We don't just want to re-create a place, we want to show our audience what we think is special about that place and what it feels like to actually be there.

To that effect, the elements brought into a theatrically designed space are carefully chosen to evoke moods, rather than to be simply a visual encyclopedia. There is always a sense of spirit and personality—be it timelessness, grandeur, elegance, bustling activity, or serenity. It is less important to use every single recognizable structure than it is to piece together an appropriate mix of primary, secondary, and tertiary components that work together properly.

Every designer maintains a mental catalog of imagery based upon various reactions on the part of the viewer. We study the tendencies people have in the way they respond to visual images placed before them. These tendencies, merged with the results of the extensive research we do, become a language of visual communication by which we set the scene for the stories we want to tell.

113

The top of the Eiffel Tower peeks over the skyline of our Paris.

Scaling Great Heights

France is another perfect place to emphasize WDI's more traditional use of forced perspective. This theatrical design device is commonly used by Imagineers in order to make our theme park spaces feel appropriately grand. The Eiffel Tower that rises above the roofline of our little representation of Paris proves this point succinctly.

Much like Cinderella Castle at Magic Kingdom Park, the Eiffel Tower is designed so that it appears to be much taller than we were able to build it. We add to this the desire to make it appear farther away than it really is, in order for this apparent height to be believable.

The tower itself is constructed at one-tenth the size of the Parisian original. All details are scaled down appropriately, so that no little piece is out of context to spoil the illusion. Because the base of our tower is not visible from the promenade, we also have to account for the fact that the tower is supposed to be a mile or so away from your vantage point. This is the only way for our tower to pass for one that is over a thousand feet tall. To that end, we didn't build the lower reaches of the tower, as sight lines would never allow the viewer to see those parts over the nearby rooftops. Had we built an entire miniaturized tower and plopped it down on top of the buildings, the effect would have given itself away because it wouldn't have taken into consideration the Guests' point of view.

United Nations

It's very important that each of the participants in World Showcase have similar presence here, and forced perspective is one of the tools that allows us to maintain our theatrical diplomacy. The iconic landmarks that define our skyline are each rendered at a different scale, in order to accomplish this balancing act, while producing a vista within which each nation carries just about the same visual weight. After these adjustments in scale have been made, we have to treat each element independently with regards to forced perspective. These examples can be found throughout World Showcase. From the pyramid at Mexico that appears to be much taller than its thirty-six feet to the Campanile in Italy passing for one that is fifty feet tall, these tricks ensure that World Showcase pavilions hint at the grandeur of the source material.

The Farthest Distance Between Two Points . . .

Another application of forced perspective can be seen in this photo of the Japan pavilion, taken from the garden behind the pagoda. The perceived distance to the rooftop visible over the Yakitori House is derived from a combination of real distance—owing to the layout of the pavilion around a central courtyard—and implied distance gained by altering the scale of the far-off building and its surface treatments.

One of the towers of Shirasagi-Jo as seen beyond Yakitori House at Japan

This study sketch by Harry Webster demonstrates the relationship between the Eiffel Tower and the rest of the typical Parisian streetscape. The tower can be seen from great distances because it is significantly taller than most of the other structures in town. However, you can't see the base of the tower from your point of view, so we have to take this into account when we plan our forced perspective.

Concept rendering of the China Kidcot location by Dave Minichiello

World Travel—It's Not Just for Grown-ups Anymore

The Kidcot program for Epcot was launched in World Showcase as a means of bringing our younger travellers into contact with the wonderful Cast Members from all around the world who staff these pavilions under the auspices of Epcot's World Fellowship Program. They come here for a one-year commitment to work in the Park and bring our Guests some insight into the people of each country. One of the greatest resources to teach our visitors about the places represented here is our cadre of cultural ambassadors who come here to meet the world.

Kidcots began life as little activity centers provided to give another level of activity for the kids who come to the Park. The concept was plussed into something much more connected to the countries of origin. The venues were developed into an appropriate look for each nation, with facilities designed to be kid-sized and fitted to each activity. The decor was chosen to reflect the nature of the craft being performed. Children take with them a craftwork mask and add new pieces as they make their way around the lagoon and participate in all the activities. This provides for them a souvenir of their experiences. Their sense of accomplishment is palpable. It's made World Showcase even more accessible to an entire category of Guests.

Early concepts for Mexico and Morocco Kidcots by Dave Minichiello

The initial Kidcot logo concept thumbnail and the finished graphic design, both by Jason Grandt

Very Blair

The logo for Kidcot is the one common element throughout the graphic system. It serves to identify each location for those seeking them out, as well as providing a means of quickly communicating the program in our guide books and other materials. This image was clearly inspired by the work of Imagineer Mary Blair, whose style led the way for "it's a small world." Her work designing for children—in the fields of animation, theme park design, and book illustration—makes her the perfect touchstone for an image intended to celebrate children around the world.

Variety Is the Spice of Life

Often when we design multiple iterations of the same thing, as with Kidcots around the World Showcase, we want to find ways to differentiate each one so that they have an individual identity.

Marquee graphic designs for Morocco (above), Mexico (left), and Norway (below), by Jason Grandt

These concepts for the Kidcots at Norway, Mexico, and Morocco illustrate the ways in which this is accomplished.

117

The streets of the United Kingdom illustrated by Group West

A Jolly Holiday

Our trip through the United Kingdom is a trip through time. There is a progression through time and around the kingdom built into the building facades and interior spaces that line our streets. Traveling from left to right on the promenade, we begin with the 1500s, represented by The Tea Caddy. Its thatched roof and half-timbered walls are modeled after Anne Hathaway's cottage at Stratford-Upon-Avon. We move into the 1600s with The Queen's Table—a two-story structure with gable barge boards, diamond-shaped wooden moldings, trefoils, clovers, and chevrons. Its Queen Anne Room, rendered all in plaster, takes us to the 1700s. Lords and Ladies stands in for the 1800s, with its exterior of dressed stone and pedimented four-column center leading up to the stone balustered parapet at the roofline. In order to tie it all together, we return to the 1500s as we make our way from The Toy Soldier past The Crown & Crest to Sportsman's Shoppe—modeled on Hampton Court on the east facade and Walter Scott's Abbotsford Manor on the south face. This treatment allows for a broad, sweeping vision of the United Kingdom that holds together as a single piece.

QUICK TAKES

• The crests seen on the windows of Sportsman's Shoppe represent the four regions of the United Kingdom—England, Scotland, Northern Ireland, and Wales. When the first three are overlaid, they form the Union Jack flag of the United Kingdom.

• The motto of the Rose & Crown, seen on the entrance sign and on the menus, is *"Otium cum Dignitate,"* Latin for "Leisure with Dignity."

• The facades on the back side of the butterfly garden overlooking Britannia Square were taken from set drawings from *Mary Poppins*.

The Rose & Crown and its many styles are ably rendered by Tom Gilleon

A Pub, by Any Other Name...

The Rose & Crown, our traditional British pub, actually corrals four different styles of pubs prevalent in different reaches of the United Kingdom. All make an appearance on the exterior of the building, and each corresponds to a similarly styled space inside.

• The city, or "street," pub dating from the 1890s Victorian city center—features brick and wood paneling on the facade and gives us our elegant mahogany bar, the etched glass, and the molded plaster ceiling.

• Dickensian pub, after the Cheshire Cheese pub in London—offers a brick-walled flagstone terrace with covered tables, a slate roof, and half-timbered, Elizabethan-styled exterior.

• Waterfront, or "river," pub, on the canal lock—a facade with a modest stone building, a clay tile roof and decorative doorways, stone terrace with an iron fence lining the homey village-inn–styled dining room.

• Country, "provincial," pub, from the suburbs of the 17th and 18th centuries—a slate roof and plaster exterior with stone-quoined corners.

Variety is important in our designs, even for spaces found somewhat off the beaten path. This small stretch of facade on a side street features four different types of brick, stone and plaster surface treatments, four different styles of architectural ornamentation, and three different roof materials, in addition to crests, graphics, themed lighting fixtures, and window treatments.

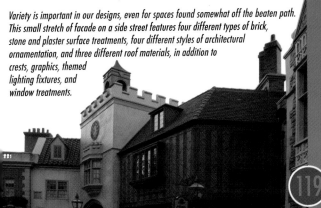

Overview of the Canadian pavilion by Bill Sully

Northern Neighbors

The challenge in telling the story of Canada, as with many of our participants in World Showcase, is to somehow capture the breadth and variety of the nation itself. Canada is a vast space, with a fascinating range of cultural histories and geographical diversity. Our pavilion works hard to do justice to this wonderful place and to demonstrate its majesty from coast to coast.

To begin with, we subdivided the pavilion into individual components that capture the sense of some of those settings. We start with the beauty and serenity of Victoria Gardens, inspired by Butchart Gardens near Victoria, British Columbia. This garden, fashioned by Jennie Butchart—the wife of concrete-industry pioneer Robert Butchart—from an abandoned limestone quarry, is considered one of the most beautiful botanical parks in the world. Our landscapers acclimated the plants here for two years before the Park opened so that they were prepared to withstand the Florida weather. Then we see the Hotel du Canada, the large limestone building with the 19th-century chateau-style Victorian architecture. This hotel is emblematic of the pioneering march West across the Canadian frontier as well as the English and French influence on the architecture. Next we arrive at that frontier, illustrated here by the Northwest Mercantile and the Trading Post, which show the influence of the Indians of the Northwest Coast, with its rough-hewn structures and prominent totem poles. At the top of the steps, we move into a smaller village around the base of the hotel, reminiscent of the charming maritime provinces of Prince Edward Island, Nova Scotia, and New Brunswick. From here we are afforded our most striking view of Salmon Island—an oasis in the heart of the Rocky Mountains, which hints at the incredible beauty of the untamed wilderness of Canada and serves as a picturesque backdrop for the entire pavilion.

The Rocky Mountains of Canada peeking over Victoria Gardens

Making a Mountain Out of a ... Smaller Mountain

Even our version of the Rocky Mountains gets the forced-perspective treatment here. These peaks, as massive as they may appear to be, could not be built at anything like actual size. In order to maximize their impact, we employed the typical practices of forced perspective. This bag of tricks can be applied to organic forms in addition to architectural features. All of the same principles are brought to bear. Mountain peaks that are farther away are reduced in scale relative to those in the foreground. Details in the rock work and the character paint are held back on the distant surfaces in order to imply atmospheric perspective—the distance that is perceived by our eyes as light passes through more air and picks up less detail. Plant material is chosen so as to maintain the illusion of distance and height. These techniques would be built upon over the years and put to even greater use much later in the imagineering of Mount Prometheus at Tokyo DisneySea and Expedition Everest at Disney's Animal Kingdom.

This totem, carved by the artist David Boxley, was a WDI enhancement effort. This project involved a performance element as well as a physical addition to the pavilion. Mr. Boxley came to Florida in 1998 and carved this totem pole onstage at Canada, generating wonderful interaction with Guests, as well as a sense on their part of having seen an element of the Park come into being.

Whoa... Canada!

Canada fits the mold of the rest of our World Showcase nations in that it's difficult harnessing all the research done into a reasonably sized theme park presentation. Canada, like China, is an ideal candidate for the Circle-Vision treatment, as it is just too vast to capture on just one screen. The range of scenery, the scope of the architecture, and the charm of the people warrants a good many more screens than that!

That variety—in both the people and the places—became the underlying theme for the project's producers. They visited all twelve provinces, filming for almost two years in order to capture all the events they hoped to show while working around the intermittent cooperation of the Canadian weather. More than a quarter of a million feet of film was shot—remember, every minute filmed must be multiplied times nine!

This proved to be one of the most challenging shoots the Circle-Vision system has ever been put through. The weather certainly was a major concern, as there were a number of aerial shoots required. The rig was mounted beneath helicopters and in the bomb bay of a B-25 for the flyover shots. On land, it was fitted to a toboggan, a dogsled, a racing chuck wagon, dollies, and flatbed trucks. Just to round out the effort, it made an appearance on several ships and boats, including the schooner *Bluenose II*.

The cameras were also subjected to temperatures of twenty-four degrees below zero at the hockey game and a wind-chill factor of fifty below during one of the helicopter shoots. The conditions were so harsh that the cameras needed to be warmed by electric heaters periodically so that they could shoot for short bursts before being set up to warm again.

The results of all this hardship were worth it, however, as the crew of six returned with fantastic footage from all across this great land—the harbors at Lunenberg, Nova Scotia, and Vancouver, the snow-crested mountains and Kaskawulsh Glacier in the Yukon Territory, and Tuktoyaktuk Peninsula in the Northwest Territories.

How We Approach Our Films

Pre-shows are very important to WDI, and go a long way toward enhancing an experience for our Guests. It can put them into a particular mood or provide them with helpful background information that will ensure that all the elements of the show make sense.

A pre-show, however, can begin before you even get to the doors of an attraction. As we see in Canada, the path you traverse to get to those doors begins to tell the story. As we make our way past the Hotel du Canada and the Maritime Provinces, we find ourselves in a lush Rocky Mountain grotto with a rushing waterfall. The stone stairway with rustic handrails give us a tactile sense of where we are and where we're going. The setting of the queue space takes this idea even farther. By the time we start the film, we've already been given a sense of all the parts of the country we're about to see.

Interior wall elevation by Barb Dietzel

Night Light

All of our parks are designed to look great at night. Our lighting designers work very hard to show off the hard work done by the rest of us. They use light to paint the parks at night and to bring them to life with a special kind of magic and energy. World Showcase is especially successful in this regard. The charm of the international facades, the reflections off of the World Showcase Lagoon,

United Kingdom at night by Bob Scif

and the added effect of nighttime shows such as IllumiNations: Reflections of Earth transform World Showcase into another place entirely.

Our concept illustrators often produce versions of their drawings showing what an idea might look like lit up at night. This is a practice dating all the way back to the great bird's-eye view of Disneyland by Peter Ellenshaw that was painted with white light paint for the daytime view and glow-in-the-dark paint to show off the look of the evening hours. These concepts show how we might maintain the focal points and how a feature piece such as a fountain or kinetic sculpture might look under the lights. A wienie still has to function as a wienie, even at night.

Our lighting designers accomplish this through very careful prior planning. Before construction they specify to us where they will need to locate uplights for building facades or landscape elements, where they will want to place lighting on the architecture of the buildings to allow for highlighting or lighting effects such as chase patterns, and where they need to place theatrical fixtures to light major park elements from a distance. This is all in addition to the placement of practical lighting fixtures that become part of the set design in addition to their lighting function. Clearly, it's very important for them to be able to visualize this effort in advance, as the tools of their trade require that electricity and control wiring be run to the location, and that support brackets be integrated into the building designs. The coordination between Imagineering disciplines required to pull off this and other sorts of integration efforts is critical.

As seen in this nighttime view of Germany, the inherent charm of the pavilions of World Showcase is only enhanced by the careful application of warm lighting and the appropriate character-lighting fixtures being put to good use. This presents a welcoming face to passersby, inviting everyone in for a closer look.

Nighttime spectaculars like IllumiNations are not WDI productions, but rather the work of the talented artists of Walt Disney Entertainment. We do assist them, however, by providing the canvas upon which they do their work. In this case, of course, WDI built the buildings, providing the surfaces for their projection and lighting designers to play with. In addition, we assist with infrastructure such as drawbridges for access, speaker shrouds, projector positions, and the noteworthy torches that were added for the Millennium edition of the show. This type of interaction between departments is an important part of the show.

We hope you've enjoyed this tour of Epcot as much as we have. Now, you can see the Park through the eyes of an Imagineer. Look for these and so many other little gems hidden in plain sight all throughout the Park. Have fun rediscovering this fabulous place. But most of all, we hope you . . .

Enjoy the Park!

BIBLIOGRAPHY

The Art of Walt Disney, Christopher Finch, Harry N. Abrams, Inc., 1973, rev. 1995, 2004

A Brush with Disney—An Artist's Journey, told through the words and works of Herbert Dickens Ryman, edited by Bruce Gordon and David Mumford, Camphor Tree Publishers, 2000

Building a Dream: The Art of Disney Architecture, Beth Dunlop, Harry N. Abrams, Inc., 1996

Designing Disney: Imagineering and the Art of the Show, John Hench with Peggy Van Pelt, Disney Editions, 2003

Designing Disney's Theme Parks: The Architecture of Reassurance, Karal Ann Marling, Flammarion/CCA, 1997

Disney A to Z: The Official Encyclopedia, Dave Smith, Hyperion, 1996, rev. 1998, 2006

Disney: The First 100 Years, Dave Smith and Steven Clark, Hyperion, 1999, rev. 2002

Disneyland, Martin A. Sklar, Walt Disney Productions, 1963

Disneyland: Dreams, Traditions and Transitions, Leonard Shannon, Disney's Kingdom Editions, 1994

Disneyland: The Inside Story, Randy Bright, Harry N. Abrams, Inc., 1987

Disneyland: The Nickel Tour, David Mumford and Bruce Gordon, Camphor Tree Publishers, 1995

Remembering Walt: Favorite Memories of Walt Disney, Amy Boothe Green and Howard E. Green, Disney Editions, 1999

Since the World Began, Jeff Kurtti, Hyperion, 1996

The Story of Walt Disney World, Walt Disney Productions, 1978

Walt Disney Imagineering: A Behind the Dreams Look at Making the Magic Real, The Imagineers, Hyperion, 1996

Walt Disney World: 20 Magical Years, The Walt Disney Company, 1991

Walt Disney's Epcot: Creating the New World of Tomorrow, Richard R. Beard, Harry N. Abrams, Inc., 1982

Walt's Time: From Before to Beyond, Robert B. Sherman and Richard M. Sherman, Camphor Tree Publishers, 1998

Kinetics - Movement and motion in a scene that give it life and energy. This can come from moving vehicles, active signage, changes in the lighting, special effects, or even hanging banners or flags that move around as the wind blows.

Maquette - A model, especially a sculpture, depicting a show element in miniature scale so that design issues can be worked out before construction begins. It's much easier to make changes on a maquette than on a full-size anything.

Plan - A direct overhead view of an object or a space. Very useful in verifying relative sizes of elements and the flow of Guests and show elements through an area.

Plussing - A word derived from Walt's penchant for always trying to make an idea better. Imagineers are continually trying to *plus* their work, even after it's "finished."

POV - Point Of View. The position from which something is seen, or the place an artist chooses to use as the vantage point of the imaginary viewer in a concept illustration. POVs are chosen in order to best represent the idea being shown.

Propping - The placement of objects around a scene. From books on a shelf to place settings on a table to wall hangings in an office space, props are the elements that give a set life and describe the people who live there. They are the everyday objects we see all around but that point out so much about us if you pay attention to them.

Section - A drawing that looks as if it's a slice through an object or space. This is very helpful in seeing how various elements interrelate. It is typically drawn as though it were an elevation, with heavier line weights defining where our imaginary cut would be.

Show - Everything we put "onstage" in a Disney park. Walt believed that everything we put out for the Guests in our parks was part of a big show, so much of our terminology originated in the show business world. With that in mind, *show* becomes for us a very broad term that includes just about anything our Guests see, hear, smell, or come in contact with during their visit to any of our Parks or Resorts.

Story - Story is the fundamental building block of everything WDI does. Imagineers are, above all, storytellers. The time, place, characters, and plot points that give our work meaning start with the story, which is also the framework that guides all design decisions.

Storyboard - A large pin-up board used to post ideas in a charrette or to outline the story points of a ride or film. The technique was perfected by Walt in the early days of his animation studio and became a staple of the animated film development process. The practice naturally transferred over to WDI when so many of the early Imagineers came over from Walt's Animation department.

Theme - The fundamental nature of a story in terms of what it means to us, or the choice of time, place, and decor applied to an area in order to support that story.

THRC - Theoretical Hourly Ride Capacity. The number of guests per hour that can experience an attraction under optimal conditions. THRC is always taken into account when a new attraction is under consideration.

Visual Intrusion - Any outside element that makes its way into a scene, breaks the visual continuity, and destroys the illusion. WDI works hard to eliminate visual intrusions.

Wienie - Walt's playful term for a visual element that could be used to draw people into and around a space. A wienie is big enough to be seen from a distance and interesting enough to make you want to take a closer look, like Spaceship Earth at the entrance to Epcot, or the Eiffel Tower in France. Wienies are critical to our efforts at laying out a sequence of experiences in an organized fashion.

Imagineering Lingo

WDI has a very vibrant and unique culture, which is even embodied in the terms we throw around the office when we're working. Here is a guide to help you understand us a bit better as we show you around the Park.

Area Development - The interstitial spaces between the attractions, restaurants, and shops. This would include landscape architecture, propping, show elements, and special enhancements intended to expand the experience.

Audio-Animatronics - The term for the three-dimensional animated human and animal characters we employ to perform in our shows and attractions. Audio-Animatronics was invented by Imagineers at Walt's request, and is an essential piece in the process in the development of many iconic Disney attractions.

Berm - A raised earthen barrier, typically heavily landscaped, which serves to eliminate visual intrusions into the Park from the outside world and block the outside world from intruding inside.

BGM - Background Music. The musical selections that fill in the audio landscape as you make your way around the Park. Each BGM track is carefully selected, arranged, and recorded to enhance the story being told.

Blue Sky - The early stages in the idea-generation process when anything is possible. There are not yet any considerations taken into account that might rein in the creative process. At this point, the sky's the limit!

Brainstorm - A gathering for the purpose of generating as many ideas as possible in the shortest time possible. We hold many brainstorming sessions at WDI, always looking for the best ideas. Imagineering has a set of Brainstorming Rules, which are always adhered to.

> **Rule 1-** There is no such thing as a bad idea. We never know how one idea (however far-fetched) might lead into another one that is exactly right.
> **Rule 2-** We don't talk yet about *why not*. There will be plenty of time for realities later, so we don't want them to get in the way of the good ideas now.
> **Rule 3-** Nothing should stifle the flow of ideas. No buts or can'ts, or other "stopping" words. We want to hear words such as "and," "or," and "what if?"
> **Rule 4-** There is no such thing as a bad idea. (We take that one very seriously.)

Charrette - Another term for a brainstorming session. From the French word for "cart." It refers to the cart sent through the Latin Quarter in Paris to collect the art and design projects of students at the legendary École des Beaux-Arts who were unable to deliver them to the school themselves after the mad rush to complete their work at the end of the term.

Concept - An idea and the effort put into communicating it and developing it into something usable. A concept can be expressed as a drawing, a written description, or simply a verbal pitch. Everything we do starts out as a concept.

Dark Ride - A term often used to describe the charming little Fantasyland attractions housed more or less completely inside a show building, which allows for greater isolation of show elements and light control, as needed.

Elevation - A drawing of a true frontal view of an object—usually a building—often drawn from multiple sides, eliminating the perspective that you would see in the real world, for clarity in the design and to lead construction activities.

E-Ticket - The top level of attractions. This dates back to an early Disneyland ticketing system used to distribute ridership through all attractions in the Park. Each was assigned a letter (A,B,C,D,E) indicating where it fell in the Park's pecking order.

Special Effects creates all of the magical (but also totally believable) smoke, fire, lightning, ghosts, explosions, pixie dust, water, wind, rain, snow, and sparks that give our stories action and a sense of surprise. Some of these effects are quite simple, while others rely on the most sophisticated technologies that can be drawn from the field of entertainment or any other imaginable industry.

Even a waterfall is a special effect in a Disney park.

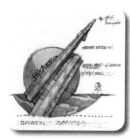

Production Design starts with the show design, takes it to the next level of detail, and ensures that it can be built so as to maintain the creative intent. It also has the task of integrating the show with all the other systems that will need to be coordinated in the field during installation.

Master Planning looks into the future and maps out the best course of action for laying out all of our properties for development. In fact, they see farther into the future than any other Imagineering division, often working with an eye toward projects that might be many years away from realization.

R&D stands for Research & Development. WDI R&D is the group that gets to play with the coolest toys. They investigate all the latest technologies from every field of study and look for ways to apply them to Disney entertainment, often inventing new ways to utilize those developments. R&D serves as a resource for the entire company.

Project Management is responsible for organizing our teams, schedules, and processes so that our projects can be delivered when they're supposed to be, within a financial framework and at the expected level of quality.

Construction Management ensures that every job meets the Disney construction standards, including quality control, code compliance, and long-term durability during operation.

Landscape Architecture is the discipline that focuses on our tree and plant palette and area development. This includes the layout of all of our hardscape and the arrangement of foliage elements on and between attractions.

Show Set Design takes concepts and breaks them down into bite-size pieces that are organized into drawing and drafting packages, integrated into the architectural, mechanical, civil, or other components of the project, and tracked during fabrication.

Show set design by Jim Heffron

Character Paint creates the reproductions of various materials, finishes, and states of aging whenever we need to make something new look old.

Character Plaster produces the hard finishes in the Park that mimic other materials. This includes rock work, themed paving, and architectural facades such as faux stone and plaster. They even use concrete to imitate wood!

Dimensional Design is the art of model making and sculpture. This skill is used to work out design issues ahead of time in model form, ensuring that our relative scales and spatial relationships are properly coordinated. Models are a wonderful tool for problem-solving.

Fabrication Design involves developing and implementing the production strategies that allow us to build all the specialized items on the large and complex projects that we deliver. Somebody has to figure out how to build the impossible!

Lighting Design puts all the hard work the rest of us have done on our shows and attractions into the best light. Lighting designers are also responsible for specifying all of the themed lighting fixtures found in the parks. As our lighting designers are fond of telling us, "without lights, it's radio!"

The Land marquee designed by Kyle Miller

Graphic Designers produce signage, both flat and dimensional, in addition to providing lots of the artwork, patterns, and details that finish the Disney show. Marquees and directional signs are just a couple of examples of their work.

Prop Design is concerned with who "lives" in a given area of a park. All of the pieces and parts of everyday life that tell you about a person or a location are very carefully selected and placed. These props have to be found, purchased, prepped, built, and installed.

Propping on the lagoon wall in France

Sound Designers work to develop the auditory backdrop for everything you see and experience. Sound is one of the most evocative senses. The songs in the attractions, the background music in the lands, and the sound effects built into show elements all work together to complete our illusions.

Media Design creates all of the various film, video, audio, and on-screen interactive content in our parks. Theme Park Productions, Inc. (TPP), a sister company to WDI, serves as something of an in-house production studio.

Screen image from Mission: SPACE

9

WDI Disciplines

Imagineers form a diverse organization, with over 140 different job titles working toward the common goal of telling great stories. WDI has an exceptionally broad collection of disciplines considering its size, due to the highly specialized nature of our work. In everything it does, WDI is supported by many other divisions of The Walt Disney Company.

American Adventure concept by Joe Warren

Show/Concept Design and Illustration produces the early drawings and renderings that serve as the inspiration for our projects and provides the initial concepts and visual communication. This artwork gives the entire team a shared vision.

Show Writing develops the stories we want to tell in the parks, as well as any nomenclature that is required. This group writes the scripts for our attractions, the copy for plaques, and names our lands, rides, shops, vehicles, and restaurants.

Architecture is responsible for turning those fanciful show drawings into real buildings, meeting all of the functional requirements that are expected of them. Our parks present some unique architectural challenges.

Interior fixtures at MouseGear

Interior Designers are responsible for the design details on the inside of our buildings. They develop the look and feel of interior spaces, and select finishes, furniture, and fixtures to complete the design.

Engineering disciplines at WDI set our mechanical, electrical, and other standards and make all of our ideas work. Engineers design structures and systems for our buildings, bridges, ride systems, and play spaces, and solve the tricky problems we throw their way every day.

The Dreaming Continues

Today's Imagineering is a vast and varied group, involved in projects all over the world in every stage of development, from initial conception right through to installation and even beyond that into support and constant improvement efforts. In addition to our headquarters in Glendale, California, near the company's Burbank studios, Imagineers are based at all field locations around the world. Additionally, WDI serves as a creative resource for the entire Walt Disney Company, bringing new ideas and new technologies to all of our storytellers.

Okay, Here's the Résumé

To date, Imagineers have built eleven Disney theme parks, a town, two cruise ships, dozens of resort hotels, water parks, shopping centers, sports complexes, and various entertainment venues worldwide. Some specific highlights include:

- Disneyland (1955)
- Magic Kingdom Park (1971)
- *Epcot* ® (1982)
- Tokyo Disneyland (1983)
- Disney Studios (1989)
- Typhoon Lagoon (1989)
- Pleasure Island (1989)
- Disneyland Resort Paris (1992)
- Town of Celebration (1994)
- Blizzard Beach (1995)
- Disney's Animal Kingdom Park (1998)
- DisneyQuest (1998)
- Disney Cruise Line (*Magic* 1998, *Wonder* 1999)
- ABC Times Square Studios (2000)
- Disney's California Adventure Park (2001)
- Tokyo DisneySea (2001)
- Walt Disney Studios Park (2002)
- Hong Kong Disneyland (2005)

He's on Our Name Tags

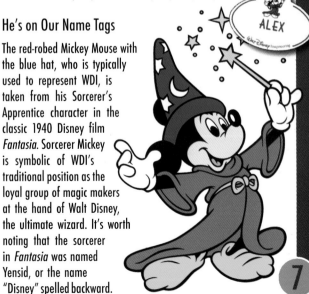

The red-robed Mickey Mouse with the blue hat, who is typically used to represent WDI, is taken from his Sorcerer's Apprentice character in the classic 1940 Disney film *Fantasia*. Sorcerer Mickey is symbolic of WDI's traditional position as the loyal group of magic makers at the hand of Walt Disney, the ultimate wizard. It's worth noting that the sorcerer in *Fantasia* was named Yensid, or the name "Disney" spelled backward.

7

A Brief History of Imagineering

Walt Disney walking the site where he planned to begin building his city of tomorrow

The Ultimate Workshop

Walt Disney Imagineering (WDI) is the design and development arm of The Walt Disney Company. "Imagineering" is Walt Disney's combination of the words *imagination* and *engineering*, pointing out the combination of skills embodied by the group. Imagineers are responsible for designing and building Disney parks, resorts, cruise ships, and other entertainment venues. WDI is a highly creative organization, with a broad range of skills and talents represented. Disciplines range from writers to architects, artists to engineers, and cover all the bases in-between. Imagineers are playful, dedicated, and abundantly curious.

Walt was our first Imagineer, but as soon as he began developing the early ideas for Disneyland, he started recruiting others to help him realize his dream. He snapped up several of his most trusted and versatile animators and art directors to apply the skills of filmmaking to the three-dimensional world. They approached this task much the same as they would a film project. They wrote stories, drew storyboards, created inspirational art, assigned the production tasks to the various film-based disciplines, and built the whole thing from scratch. Disneyland is essentially a movie that allows you to walk right in and join in the fun. As Imagineer par excellence John Hench was fond of saying in response to recent trends, "Virtual reality is nothing new . . . we've been doing that for more than fifty years!"

WDI was founded on December 16, 1952, under the name WED Enterprises (from the initials **W**alter **E**lias **D**isney). Imagineering has been an integral part of the the company's culture ever since. Imagineers are the ones who ask the "what ifs?" and "why nots?" that lead to some of our most visible and most beloved landmarks. Collectively, the Disney parks have become the physical embodiment of all that our company's mythologies represent to kids of all ages.

TABLE OF CONTENTS

For information address Disney Editions, 114 Fifth Avenue, New York, New York 10011–5690.

Printed in Singapore

The following are trademarks, registered marks, and service marks owned by Disney Enterprises, Inc.: Adventureland® Area, Audio-Animatronics®, Circle-Vision, Disney®, Disneyland® Park, Disneyland® Resort, Disneyland® Resort Paris, Disney Studios, Disney's Animal Kingdom® Theme Park, Disney's California Adventure® Park, Epcot®, Expedition Everest, Fantasyland® Area, Frontierland® Area, Future World, Imagineering, Imagineers, "it's a small world," Magic Kingdom® Park, Main Street, U.S.A.® Area, monorail, Space Mountain® Attraction, Splash Mountain® Attraction, Tokyo Disneyland® Park, Tokyo DisneySea®, Tomorrowland® Area, Walt Disney World® Resort, World Showcase

Finding Nemo characters © Disney Enterprises, Inc. and Pixar Animation Studios

The Twilight Zone® is a registered trademark of CBS, Inc., and is used pursuant to a license from CBS, Inc.

Indiana Jones™ Adventure © Disney/Lucasfilm, Ltd.

For Disney Editions
Editorial Director: Wendy Lefkon
Senior Editor: Jody Revenson

Written and Designed by Alex Wright with help from all the Imagineers

For Mom & Dad, for daydreaming about EPCOT

The author would like to thank Jason Surrell for his ongoing support; Scott Otis for the continued use of his extensive Disney library; Jim Snyder, Greg Randle, and Jason Grandt for help with the legwork; Jody Revenson for her continued guidance; David Buckley for the use of his Sorcerer Mickey illustration on the cover; Gary Landrum for access to his SQS collections and for a particularly informative lunch; Marty Sklar and Tom Fitzgerald for their input and for letting him do another one of these; Max Hamano and Barbara Hastings for keeping everybody informed; Dave Smith and Robert Tieman for another thorough review; Kim, Finn, and Lincoln for giving Daddy the time to work on his book; and all Imagineers past and present for their assistance and for all the inspiration they've provided through the years.

Library of Congress Cataloging-in-Publication Data on file.

ISBN: 0-7868-4886-3

First Edition
10 9 8 7 6 5 4 3 2

The Imagineering Field Guide to

Ep🌐t

at ꒰Walt Disney World꒱

An Imagineer's-Eye Tour

By The Imagineers

DISNEP

EDITIONS

New York